Contents

The fourth grade is planning a trip to the amusement park. Calculate the amount of money needed to go on a trip.

Day Passes
Adults $12
Students $10

1 It is 38 miles between the school and the amusement park. How many miles will the round trip be?

2 It will take 2 buses to seat all the fourth-graders. How many total miles will the two buses drive? Use your answer from number 1.

3 The bus drivers must be paid for their time. They charge $16.00 the first hour and $12.00 each additional hour. If the buses leave the school at 9:00 a.m. and return at 3:00 in the afternoon, how many hours will the trip take? How much will each bus driver be paid? How much should be budgeted to pay the two bus drivers?

4 If there are 98 students and 12 adults going to the amusement park, how much should the school budget for the day passes?

5 What is the total cost of the trip to the amusement park?

A Day of Fun

Break the Code

Solve the following problems. Find the answers in the key at the bottom of the page. Write the corresponding letters on the lines below the problems. Read the completed message.

```
   5      3     10          3     25      5     30           4     50      8
 × 5    × 6    + 8        × 4    + 5    ×10    - 6         × 4    - 2    × 3
  25
```

<u>A</u> <u>N</u> <u>N</u>   <u>R</u> <u>O</u> <u>D</u> <u>E</u>   ___ ___ ___

```
  15      6                  1     13     15
 - 3    × 5    18÷3        × 6    +11    - 3
```

___ ___ ___ ___ ___ ___

```
   5     12     27                9      6      7                 5      6     18     27
 × 2    +18    - 2    16÷2      + 7    × 4    + 5       27÷9    × 1    + 6    - 10    - 11
```

___ ___ ___ ___ ___ ___ ___ ___ ___ ___ ___ ___

Key

3 = F	8 = S	16 = T	25 = A	50 = D
5 = I	10 = C	18 = N	30 = O	
6 = L	12 = R	24 = E	48 = H	

A Day of Fun

Draw a straight line to connect each numerical form with its corresponding word form.

392   W   R   eighteen

      O

1,700   P   nine hundred four

489   four hundred eighty-nine

18   S   N   fifty-two

   C   I

625   two thousand three

2,003   R   K   G   three hundred ninety-two

  B

36   E   D   six thousand three hundred twenty-nine

     Y

904   J   one thousand seven hundred

   M

52   A   six hundred twenty-five

6,329   thirty-six

Write the blue letters that are inside closed figures. These letters can be arranged into two words that tell the ride that Rachel rode first when she arrived at the amusement park. What ride did Rachel ride first?

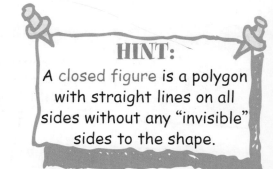

HINT:
A closed figure is a polygon with straight lines on all sides without any "invisible" sides to the shape.

K   Y   E   I   S   D

A Day of Fun

Amusement Park

Using a crayon, draw a path through the maze. At each circled number, decide if the number is odd or even and continue through the maze to the amusement park.

A Day of Fun

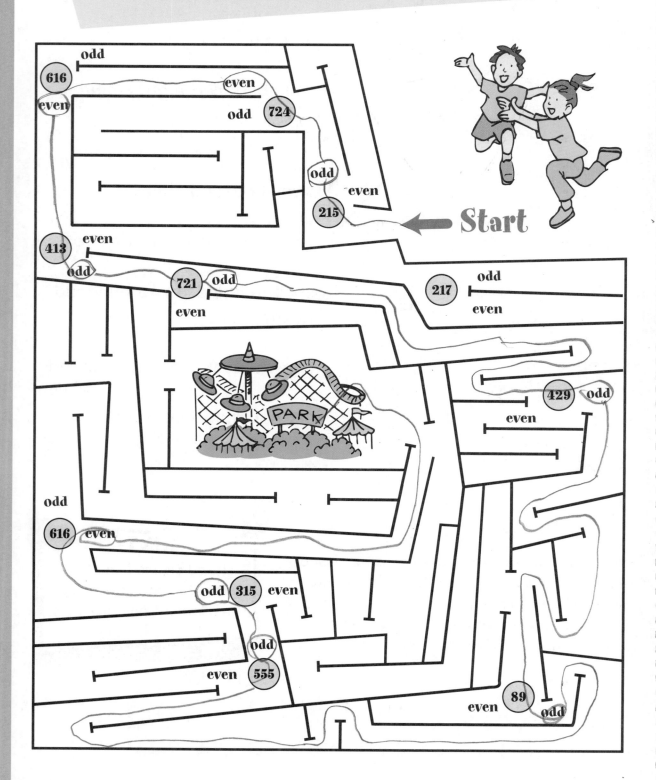

The following grid is a portion of the map of a town. The school is located at the ordered pair (5, 2). The buses start out at the school and follow the directions written at the bottom of this page to get to the amusement park. (Each square represents one city block.)

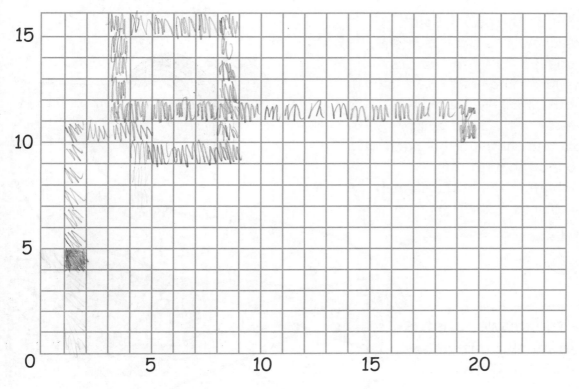

► Start at the school (5, 2).

► Go 6 blocks north.

► Go east 3 blocks to the gas station.

► Go south 1 block.

► Go east 4 blocks to the food mart.

► Go north 8 blocks.

► Go west 5 blocks to the zoo.

► Go south 5 blocks.

► Go east 16 blocks.

► Go south 1 block to the amusement park.

What is the ordered pair for each of the following?

Amusement Park _____ ?

Gas Station _____ ?

Food Mart_____ ?

Zoo _____ ?

A Day of Fun

Wonderland

A Day of Fun

North Entrance

+ 2

× 8

÷ 5

- 1

+ 24

÷ 2

+ 6

- 9

+ 15

÷ 8

Start at the park's South Entrance. The first problem reads 8 × 3. Write the first answer in the next box. Next, subtract 20. Write that answer in the next empty box, and continue this pattern around the path. After completing the path, fill in the blanks below.

Write the answer that is located by the entrance to each section of the amusement park:

Kiddie Land: _____

Lost World: _____

Treasure Land: _____

North Entrance: _____

South Entrance 8 × 3 24 - 20 × 4

When the class arrived at the amusement park, they went to see a trained seal show. The seats were arranged in the pattern below with the blue section being one cubic unit, or one cube high, and the green section being two cubes high, so the people sitting in the green section could see over the people in the blue section. How many cubes (or cubic units) were needed to make this seating area? (Don't worry about the red stage.)

Answer:

13½

cubes

Skills:

Computation

Solve the problems on the left and match them up with the answers on the right. The corresponding letters in order of the problems spell out the ride that Hernaldo rode first.

1. 12 × 4 = _____

2. 27 - 19 = _____

3.   9 × 5 = 45

4. 27 + 34 = _____

5. 30 ÷ 6 = _____

6. 17 + 6 = _____

7.   8 × 7 = _____

8. 37 - 12 = 25

9. 27 ÷ 9 = _____

10. 7 × 3 = 28

G	= 61
D	= 3
E	= 21
F	= 24
U	= 8
R	= 56
E	= 23
L	= 5
C	= 81
J	= 48
N	= 45
P	= 40
T	= 7
I	= 25
M	= 75

What ride did Hernaldo ride first?

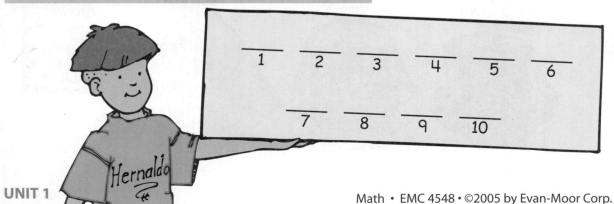

A Day of Fun

Skills:

Converting Units of Measurement

Alicia is the shortest person in fourth grade. She is only 46 inches tall and is not able to ride the Wild Thing. In order to ride the Wild Thing, riders must be 4 feet tall. How many inches away from 4 feet is Alicia? _____

Table of Conversions

1 foot = 12 inches

3 feet = 1 yard

1 mile = 5,280 feet

1 meter = 100 centimeters

1 centimeter = 10 millimeters

Compute the following conversions.

3 feet = __300__ inches

1 foot = __100__ inches

24 inches = __20__ feet

2 meters = __2,000__ centimeters

1 meter = __1,00__ centimeters

9 feet = __900__ yards

10 millimeters = __1__ centimeter

36 inches = __360__ yard

2 yards = __20__ feet

5 yards = __500__ feet

⭐ **Bonus:**

5 miles = _____ feet

A Day of Fun

Pizza for Lunch

The pizza parlor at the amusement park serves lunch every day. Look at each pizza plate and write the fraction that represents the leftover pizza.

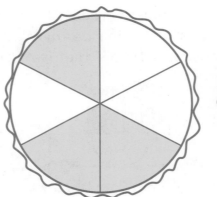

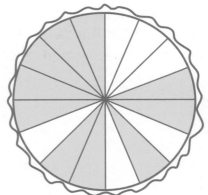

_____

_____

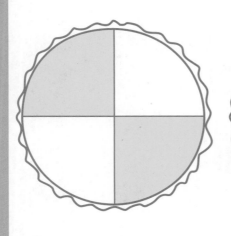

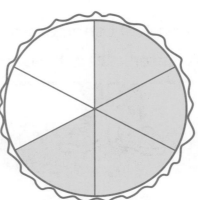

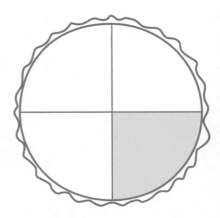

_____

_____

_____

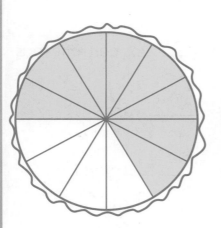

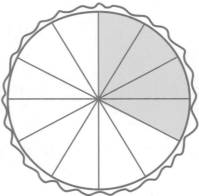

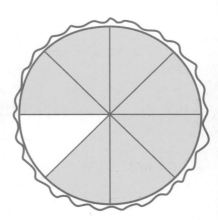

_____

_____

_____

Skills:
Computation

Check each equation and circle all the equations that are true. Complete the maze by beginning at Start and following the correct equations to the End.

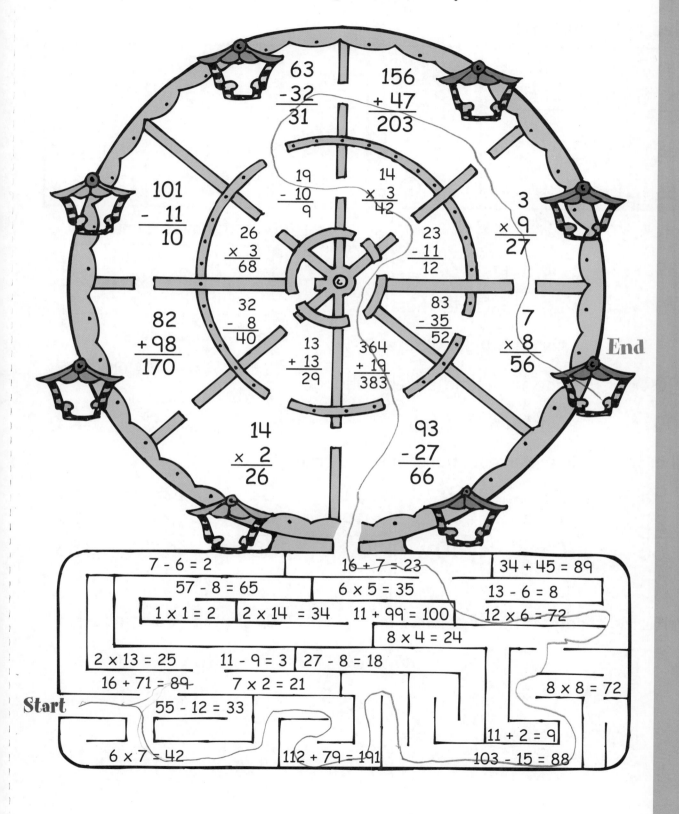

A Day of Fun

Solve the problems.

7 × 8	19 × 5	27 ÷ 9	24 ÷ 3	14 × 3	36 ÷ 6
○ 49 ○ 63	○ 14 ○ 95	○ 5 ○ 6	○ 4 ○ 8	○ 5 ○ 17	○ 9 ○ 7
○ 56 ○ 15	○ 24 ○ 45	○ 3 ○ 36	○ 6 ○ 12	○ 42 ○ 24	○ 5 ○ 6

Match.

392 •

1,700 •

18 •

904 •

2,003 •

• eighteen

• two thousand three

• three hundred ninety-two

• one thousand seven hundred

• nine hundred four

Fill in the missing number.

| 1 foot = 12 inches |
| 3 feet = 1 yard |
| 1 meter = 100 centimeters |

3 feet = _____ inches

2 meters = _____ centimeters

2 yards = _____ feet

300 centimeters = _____ meters

Fill in the circle under equations that are true.

93 - 27 66	156 + 47 203	101 - 11 10	11 + 99 100	82 + 98 180	32 - 18 20	364 + 19 383
○	○	○	○	○	○	○

Write the fraction that is colored in.

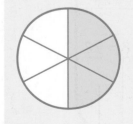

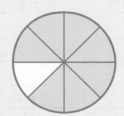

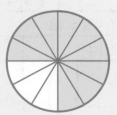

_____   _____   _____

Circle the odd numbers.

96

37

125

246

591

To Huntington Beach

There is going to be a family reunion in Huntington Beach, California. Five families are coming from five different states in the United States to attend. Solve the following problems to determine what state one of the families is coming from.

$$\begin{array}{c}10\\ \times\,7\\ \hline 70\end{array} \quad \begin{array}{c}3\\ \times\,1\end{array} \quad 16 \div 4 \qquad \begin{array}{c}9\\ \times\,5\end{array} \quad \begin{array}{c}14\\ +\,5\end{array} \quad \begin{array}{c}4\\ \times\,5\end{array} \quad \begin{array}{c}98\\ -17\end{array} \quad \begin{array}{c}1\\ \times\,4\end{array} \quad \begin{array}{c}50\\ +20\end{array} \quad \begin{array}{c}10\\ \times\,7\end{array}$$

T __ __ __   __ __ __ __ __ __ __

$$\begin{array}{c}44\\ +46\end{array} \quad \begin{array}{c}6\\ \times\,5\end{array} \quad \begin{array}{c}8\\ \times\,7\end{array} \quad \begin{array}{c}80\\ -16\end{array} \quad 7 \div 7 \quad \begin{array}{c}31\\ -\,8\end{array} \qquad \begin{array}{c}52\\ +12\end{array} \quad 27 \div 3$$

__ __ __ __ __ __   __ __

$$\begin{array}{c}11\\ \times\,5\end{array} \quad \begin{array}{c}5\\ \times\,3\end{array} \quad \begin{array}{c}50\\ +\,6\end{array} \quad \begin{array}{c}32\\ +32\end{array} \quad \begin{array}{c}91\\ -10\end{array} \quad \begin{array}{c}3\\ \times\,8\end{array} \qquad \begin{array}{c}10\\ \times\,9\end{array} \quad \begin{array}{c}14\\ +\,6\end{array} \quad 30 \div 2 \quad \begin{array}{c}67\\ -11\end{array}$$

__ __ __ __ __ __   __ __ __ __

$$\begin{array}{c}49\\ +\,7\end{array} \quad \begin{array}{c}3\\ \times\,5\end{array} \quad \begin{array}{c}75\\ +\,6\end{array} \quad \begin{array}{c}35\\ +35\end{array} \quad \begin{array}{c}41\\ -11\end{array} \quad \begin{array}{c}9\\ \times\,9\end{array} \quad \begin{array}{c}5\\ \times\,6\end{array}$$

__ __ __ __ __ __ __

Key

1 = L	15 = O	24 = G	56 = M	90 = F
3 = H	19 = U	30 = A	64 = I	
4 = E	20 = R	45 = B	70 = T	
9 = S	23 = Y	55 = C	81 = N	

Family Reunion

Draw lines of symmetry on the following figures. Then, next to each figure, write the number of lines of symmetry that figure has.

1. 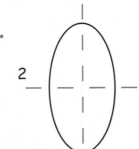 2

5. 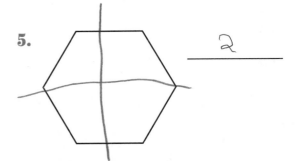 2

2. 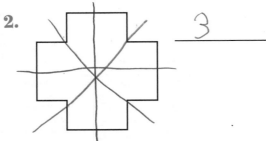 3

6. 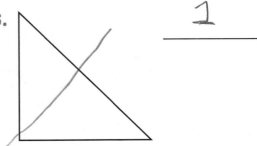 1

3.  1

7. 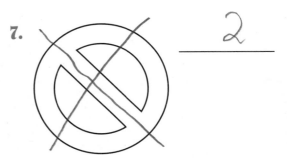 2

4. 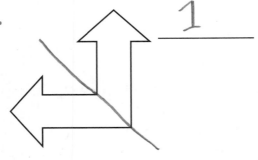 1

8. 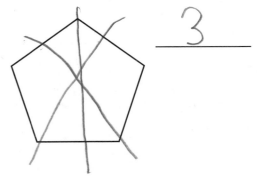 3

Math • EMC 4548 • ©2005 by Evan-Moor Corp.

Skills:

Patterning—
Figures and
Numbers

Circle the letter of the choice that would come next in each pattern. Write the answer letters in the order of the problems to answer the question at the bottom of the page.

1. 5, 10, 15, 20, _____   A) 21   B) 25   C) 30   D) 20

2. Red, Green, Green, Red,   A) Green   B) Red   C) Yellow   D) Blue
   Green, Green, Red, _____

3. † † – † † – _____   A) ®   B) ø   C) –   D) ††

4. 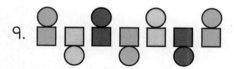   A)   B)   C)   D)

5. 7, 11, 15, 19, 23, _____   A) 27   B) 26   C) 28   D) 30

6.   A)   B)   C)   D)

7. 10, 20, 30, 40, _____   A) 40   B) 50   C) 60   D) 70

8. J, F, M, A, J, F, _____   A) M   B) A   C) J   D) D

9.   A)   B)   C)   D)

10. 38, 35, 32, 29, _____   A) 32   B) 35   C) 26   D) 20

11. $\frac{4}{8}$ ∞ △ $\frac{4}{8}$ $\frac{4}{8}$ ∞ ∞ △ △ $\frac{4}{8}$ $\frac{4}{8}$ $\frac{4}{8}$ ∞ _____   A) ∞   B) $\frac{4}{8}$ C) ©   D) △

What is the nickname of the father of the family coming from North Dakota?

Family Reunion

Skills:

Solving Word Problems

Family Reunion

One of the families travels only 280 miles to get to Huntington Beach. They live in Las Vegas, Nevada. Solve these problems about their trip.

1 The family will drive the 280 miles in their car and average about 60 miles per hour. About how many hours will they be driving?

They will be driving between

_____ hours and _____ hours.

2 Their car can go about 20 miles on every gallon of gasoline. About how many gallons of gasoline will they need to travel the 280 miles?

_____ gallons of gasoline

3 If each gallon of gas costs $1.58, about how much money will the family need for gas to travel the 280 miles?

$ _____

4 The five people in this family (2 adults and 3 kids) will stop for lunch at the Moose Restaurant. The prices are listed on the display board below. What will be the total bill without tax?

$ _____

**Moose Restaurant
All-You-Can-Eat**

Adults $7.25
Children $4.75

5 If the family has exactly $30, will they be able to pay their bill at the Moose Restaurant once they add on a $5 tip? Why or why not?

Use the digits 0 through 9 to complete these number sentences. Use each number only once. Is there more than one possible solution? _____

Skills:

Computation—
Addition,
Multiplication,
Division

0 1 2 3 4 5 6 7 8 9

□ + 5 = 11

$$\begin{array}{r} \square \\ \times\ \square \\ \hline 0 \end{array}$$

$$\begin{array}{r} 3 \\ +\ \square \\ \hline \square\ \square \end{array}$$

□ × □ = 32

15 ÷ □ = 5

Family Reunion

On the Map

This map represents the western half of the United States of America.

On this map, 1 centimeter represents about 175 miles. Use this information and a centimeter ruler to estimate the answers to the problem below.

Measure the distance from <u>Dallas</u>, Texas, to <u>Denver</u>, Colorado. About how many miles do you think it is from <u>Dallas</u> to <u>Denver</u>?

_____ cm

_____ mi.

Measure the distance from <u>Butte</u>, Montana, to <u>Dallas</u>, Texas. About how many miles do you think it is from <u>Butte</u> to Dallas?

_____ cm

_____ mi.

Measure the distance from <u>Bismarck</u>, North Dakota, to <u>Salt Lake City</u>, Utah. About how many miles do you think it is from <u>Bismarck</u> to <u>Salt Lake City</u>?

_____ cm

_____ mi.

Measure the distance from Long Beach(•), California, to <u>Bismarck</u>, North Dakota. About how many miles do you think it is from Long Beach (•) to <u>Bismarck</u>?

_____ cm

_____ mi.

Family Reunion

Plot the ordered pairs of numbers on the graph in the order in which they are listed, connecting them with straight lines. Start each new set of points with a new line.

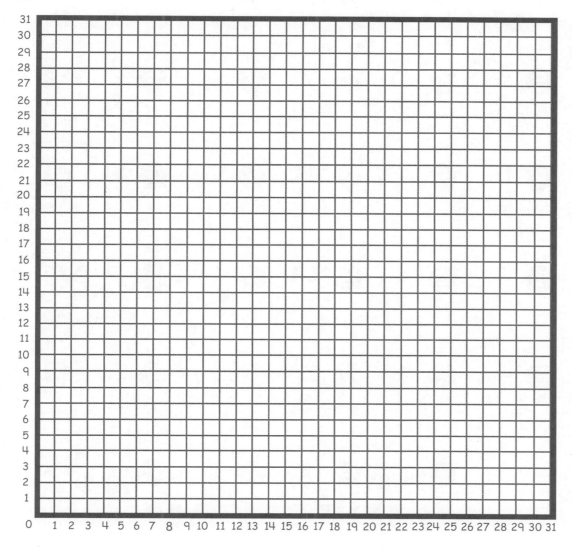

Family Reunion

HINT:

Remember that the first number of each ordered pair is for the x-axis, which is horizontal. The second number is for the y-axis, which is vertical.

The finished drawing will show an important item at the family reunion.

▶ (18, 28) (2, 23) (5, 21) (18, 28) (8, 20) (5, 21) line ends

▶ (11, 19) (18, 28) (14, 19) (11, 19) (8, 20) line ends

▶ (14, 19) (17, 19) (20, 19) (18, 28) (17, 19) (17, 2) (16, 2) (16, 19) line ends

▶ (20, 19) (23, 20) (18, 28) (26, 21) line ends

▶ (23, 20) (26, 21) (29, 23) (18, 28) line ends

▶ (0, 3) (13, 6) (20, 5) (24, 3) (28, 4) (31, 3) line ends

Skills:
Computation—
All Operations

Family Reunion

Solve these problems.

H $\begin{array}{r} 5 \\ \times 9 \\ \hline \end{array}$ **M** $\begin{array}{r} 6 \\ \times 5 \\ \hline \end{array}$ **A** $\begin{array}{r} 12 \\ - 3 \\ \hline \end{array}$ **E** $\begin{array}{r} 12 \\ + 6 \\ \hline \end{array}$ **H** $\begin{array}{r} 45 \\ + 13 \\ \hline \end{array}$ **T** $7 \div 7$

E $\begin{array}{r} 6 \\ + 5 \\ \hline \end{array}$ **T** $\begin{array}{r} 75 \\ - 15 \\ \hline \end{array}$ **Z** $\begin{array}{r} 7 \\ \times 5 \\ \hline \end{array}$ **E** $12 \div 3$ **D** $\begin{array}{r} 2 \\ \times 7 \\ \hline \end{array}$ **F** $\begin{array}{r} 39 \\ - 5 \\ \hline \end{array}$

R $\begin{array}{r} 11 \\ + 11 \\ \hline \end{array}$ **S** $27 \div 9$ **E** $\begin{array}{r} 44 \\ + 6 \\ \hline \end{array}$ **Y** $\begin{array}{r} 36 \\ - 11 \\ \hline \end{array}$ **T** $\begin{array}{r} 14 \\ - 1 \\ \hline \end{array}$ **A** $\begin{array}{r} 5 \\ \times 8 \\ \hline \end{array}$

I $\begin{array}{r} 7 \\ \times 4 \\ \hline \end{array}$ **C** $\begin{array}{r} 8 \\ \times 6 \\ \hline \end{array}$ **H** $\begin{array}{r} 59 \\ - 47 \\ \hline \end{array}$ **T** $\begin{array}{r} 14 \\ + 10 \\ \hline \end{array}$ **F** $40 \div 4$ **A** $\begin{array}{r} 8 \\ \times 4 \\ \hline \end{array}$

E $\begin{array}{r} 46 \\ - 9 \\ \hline \end{array}$ **L** $\begin{array}{r} 9 \\ \times 3 \\ \hline \end{array}$ **V** $\begin{array}{r} 53 \\ - 14 \\ \hline \end{array}$ **T** $28 \div 4$ **V** $\begin{array}{r} 5 \\ \times 4 \\ \hline \end{array}$ **E** $\begin{array}{r} 8 \\ + 7 \\ \hline \end{array}$

R $64 \div 8$ **L** $\begin{array}{r} 8 \\ \times 2 \\ \hline \end{array}$ **A** $\begin{array}{r} 35 \\ - 14 \\ \hline \end{array}$ **H** $40 \div 8$

When all the problems have been completed, write the answers in order from largest to the smallest. Then write the corresponding letter for each answer on the lines.

largest ___ ___ ___ ___ ___ ___ ___ ___

___ ___ ___ ___ ___

___ ___ ___ ___ ___ ___

___ ___ ___ ___ ___ ___ ___ **smallest**

22 UNIT 2

The digit 7 is in each of the following numbers. On the line after each number, write the place value of the 7.

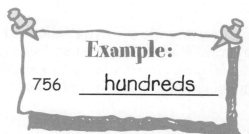

Example:

756 _____hundreds_____

7,293 _____

17 _____

2,918,736 _____

70,000 _____

279 _____

100,798 _____

796,390 _____

7,903,854 _____

38,872 _____

37,959 _____

9,895,637 _____

973 _____

7,090,836 _____

9,763 _____

ones	thousands	millions
tens	ten thousands	
hundreds	hundred thousands	

Family Reunion

Ten or Less

Skills:

Addition

Strategy

Find a partner to play the following game. Take turns crossing off one number in that row. The goal is to have the remaining numbers add up to 10 or less. If the remaining numbers add up to exactly 10, score two points for the game. If the remaining numbers add up to less than 10, score one point.

												Score
Game 1:	1	3	4	7	9	8	5	12	2	15	6	
Game 2:	15	8	6	4	9	10	7	3	1	12	2	
Game 3:	12	8	5	3	10	1	7	9	13	4	6	
Game 4:	2	4	6	8	10	12	11	9	7	5	3	
Game 5:	9	10	8	6	2	13	3	5	7	15	1	
Game 6:	8	5	1	13	7	4	14	2	3	9	16	
Game 7:	10	7	9	5	3	11	1	4	12	6	2	
Game 8:	9	4	11	8	6	3	5	14	1	15	2	
Game 9:	18	9	7	2	5	8	13	1	4	6	11	
Game 10:	1	7	6	10	16	8	4	2	13	3	5	

16–20 Expert Strategist

10–15 Good Effort

Skills:

Equalities/
Inequalities

Complete each number sentence below using one of the following symbols:

> < (Less than, for example, 7 < 8)
>
> \> (Greater than, for example, 5 > 4)
>
> = (Equal, for example, 3 = 3)

23 ◯ 29 $12.00 ◯ $12.25

14 ◯ 14   16 ◯ 29

9 ◯ 12 $9.27 ◯ $9.19

$10 ◯ $10.00   48 ◯ 38

27 ◯ 32   99 ◯ 111

84 ◯ 78   19 ◯ 15

$9.00 ◯ $9.10   43 ◯ 34

8 ◯ 12 $12.00 ◯ $12

6 ◯ 6   37 ◯ 41

48 ◯ 45 $15.73 ◯ $15.81

Family Reunion

Skills:

Logic

Complete this logic puzzle to determine where each family came from for the family reunion. Use the clues on pages 15, 17, and 22, as well as the clues at the bottom of this page.

To Huntington Beach or BUST	Colorado	Florida	Montana	Nevada	North Dakota
Bacca					
Burnett					
Chavez					
Ramos					
Smith					

Clues

Each family came from a different state.

The Bacca family is not from Montana.

The Ramos family is from Las Vegas, Nevada, or Tampa, Florida.

The Smith family is not from North Dakota.

Multiply or divide.

$$\begin{array}{r} 8 \\ \times\ 6 \\ \hline \end{array} \qquad \begin{array}{r} 5 \\ \times\ 7 \\ \hline \end{array} \qquad \begin{array}{r} 7 \\ \times\ 4 \\ \hline \end{array} \qquad \begin{array}{r} 9 \\ \times\ 5 \\ \hline \end{array}$$

64 ÷ 8 = _____   56 ÷ 7 = _____   42 ÷ 6 = _____   81 ÷ 9 = _____

Write out the number 2,856 in word form.

_____

About how many centimeters long is the following line? _____

How many inches are in 1 foot?

_____

What comes next in this pattern?

9, 15, 21, 27, 33, _____

What fraction would represent the shaded part on this bar?

_____

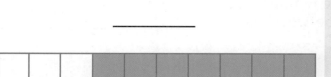

Draw the rest of this figure if the thick line represents a line of symmetry.

What place value does the 3 have in the number 53,960? _____

ASSESSMENT 2 27

A New CD

Music, Music, Music

There are five bands that have become very popular over the last few years. In August, they got together and made a CD. Each band recorded two songs. The length of each song is shown in the following table.

Song Number	Name of Band	Length of Song
1	Mississippi Mud	2 minutes 40 seconds
2	Band Five	3 minutes 15 seconds
3	Sky Way	4 minutes 10 seconds
4	Helmets	3 minutes 5 seconds
5	Top Drums	2 minutes 48 seconds
6	Mississippi Mud	3 minutes 52 seconds
7	Band Five	4 minutes 4 seconds
8	Sky Way	3 minutes 42 seconds
9	Helmets	4 minutes 22 seconds
10	Top Drums	2 minutes 30 seconds

Which band recorded the longest song, and which band recorded the shortest song?

_____

_____

Approximately how long would the CD be if you were to play the songs directly through? How did you get your estimate?

_____

_____

Exactly how long would the CD be if there was a 2-second silent break allowed between each song?

_____

_____

The company would also like to record these songs on a tape, but the order of the songs can be different. Which five songs should be put on Side A and which five songs should be put on Side B so that the two sides are equal in length?

_____

_____

Solve each problem.

1. Helena wants to buy three CD sets for the following prices: $59, $129, and $64. What will be the total cost of the three CD sets?

$_____

2. Sally would like to buy two new CDs that cost $16.99 each.

a. What will be the total cost of her purchases?

$_____

b. How much change will she get back if she pays for the CDs with two $20 bills?

$_____

3. Brandon and Ian both want to buy new stereos. Each stereo costs $229. In addition, each boy wants to buy a set of speakers for $119. The tax for the two stereos and the two sets of speakers is a total of $56. What will be the total cost for these items including tax?

$_____

Music, Music, Music

Break the Code

Solve the following problems. After solving each problem, look at the key at the bottom of the page to see what letter corresponds to the answer. Write the letter on the line below the problem. The letters will spell out a clue about how many people are in "Band Five."

$$\begin{array}{c} 9 \\ \times\ 2 \\ \hline 18 \end{array} \qquad \begin{array}{c} 3 \\ \times\ 8 \end{array} \qquad 12 \div 4 \qquad \begin{array}{c} 9 \\ \times\ 1 \end{array} \qquad\qquad \begin{array}{c} 14 \\ +16 \end{array} \qquad \begin{array}{c} 9 \\ \times\ 5 \end{array} \qquad \begin{array}{c} 46 \\ -17 \end{array} \qquad \begin{array}{c} 1 \\ \times\ 4 \end{array}$$

B ___ ___ ___ ___   ___ ___ ___ ___

$$45 \div 9 \qquad \begin{array}{c} 6 \\ \times\ 4 \end{array} \qquad \begin{array}{c} 1 \\ \times\ 6 \end{array} \qquad\qquad \begin{array}{c} 80 \\ -56 \end{array} \qquad 21 \div 7 \qquad\qquad \begin{array}{c} 12 \\ -\ 8 \end{array} \qquad \begin{array}{c} 17 \\ +12 \end{array} \qquad 16 \div 4 \qquad 27 \div 9$$

___ ___ ___   ___ ___   ___ ___ ___ ___

$$\begin{array}{c} 1 \\ \times\ 3 \end{array} \qquad \begin{array}{c} 12 \\ +\ 5 \end{array} \qquad \begin{array}{c} 58 \\ +\ 6 \end{array} \qquad \begin{array}{c} 9 \\ +\ 9 \end{array} \qquad \begin{array}{c} 91 \\ -87 \end{array} \qquad 12 \div 6 \qquad\qquad \begin{array}{c} 7 \\ \times\ 3 \end{array} \qquad \begin{array}{c} 15 \\ +15 \end{array}$$

___ ___ ___ ___ ___ ___   ___ ___

$$\begin{array}{c} 57 \\ +\ 7 \end{array} \qquad 20 \div 5 \qquad \begin{array}{c} 75 \\ -11 \end{array} \qquad \begin{array}{c} 11 \\ +\ 7 \end{array} \qquad \begin{array}{c} 41 \\ -37 \end{array} \qquad 18 \div 9 \qquad \begin{array}{c} 1 \\ \times\ 6 \end{array}$$

___ ___ ___ ___ ___ ___ ___

Key

2 = R	3 = N	4 = E	5 = H	6 = S
9 = D	17 = U	18 = B	21 = O	24 = A
29 = V	30 = F	45 = I	64 = M	

Hidden Equations

Hidden in the numbers below are at least 25 sets of numbers that can be written as an addition or subtraction problem. The addition equations may have 2 or 3 addends. The equations may read forward (left to right), down, or diagonally. Circle as many hidden problems as you can find.

2	12	98	53	28	94	88	6	12	15	37	64
3	4	11	4	6	8	80	48	93	14	79	17
6	2	6	2	17	84	5	10	32	74	28	40
7	27	4	11	51	8	9	17	29	39	5	25
4	6	17	5	28	6	26	5	45	54	4	15
3	74	16	58	4	13	7	25	8	17	93	13
5	38	6	7	9	14	53	60	73	9	17	57
8	6	5	9	14	27	86	2	29	43	18	68
9	58	12	17	12	3	4	37	44	18	17	4
4	17	13	13	9	22	37	17	16	4	97	26
1	9	37	79	27	38	16	54	29	53	59	39
5	4	7	39	46	3	28	5	86	46	38	68

Numbers & Words

Draw a straight line to connect each word form with its corresponding numerical form.

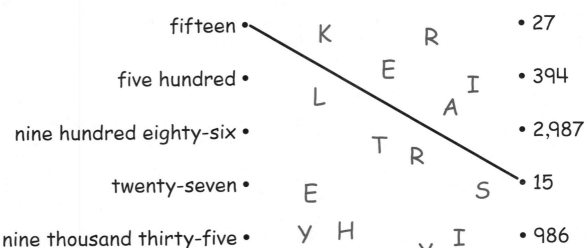

fifteen •

five hundred •

nine hundred eighty-six •

twenty-seven •

nine thousand thirty-five •

two thousand nine hundred eighty-seven •

ninety-six •

three hundred ninety-four •

one thousand eight hundred •

thirty-four •

• 27

• 394

• 2,987

• 15

• 986

• 34

• 1,800

• 500

• 9,035

• 96

Write the letters that are inside each closed figure. These letters can be arranged to create the name of a band that has nine members.

HINT:
A closed figure is a polygon with straight lines on all sides without any "invisible" sides to the shape.

Math • EMC 4548 • ©2005 by Evan-Moor Corp.

Music, Music, Music

Give the time.

When is 5 hours after 7:00 a.m.? _____	When is 20 minutes after 9:30 p.m.? _____
When is 1 hour before 10:00 a.m.? _____	When is 4 hours after 1:30 p.m.? _____
When is 15 minutes before 4:30 p.m.? _____	When is 25 minutes before 4:15 p.m.? _____
When is 20 minutes after 5:50 a.m.? _____	When is 1 hour and 15 minutes after 4:00 p.m.? _____
When is 2 hours after 11:00 a.m.? _____	When is 3 hours and 30 minutes after 4:40 a.m.? _____

Music, Music, Music

Skills:

Calculating
Volume

The picture below shows a stage that one of the bands performs on.
How many cubes does it take to create the stage?

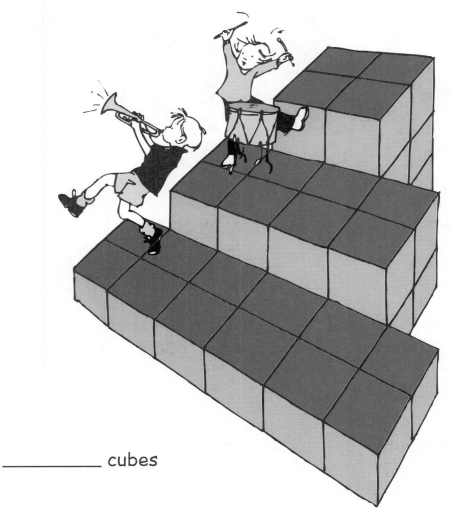

_____ cubes

⭐ Bonus: Using the same number of cubes, make a wall. Draw it here.

Take Note of Your Accuracy

Skills:

Computation—
Addition,
Subtraction,
Multiplication

Begin at Start. Compute the answer, then proceed down the path with the correct answer. When you come to ❷, do the second problem, and again continue down the path with the correct answer.

After you have completed the four problems and the maze, use the key at the bottom of the page to see how accurate you were. If you made mistakes, try again.

❶ START
56
42
35

7
$\times$ 6
?

❷ 51 - 14 = ?
❸ 26 × 4 = ?
❹ 17 + 48 = ?

43 ❷
37

43 ❷
37

43 ❷
37

❸ 104 30
❸ 30 104
❸ 30 104
❸ 30 104
❸ 30 104

30 ❹ 104
❹
❹ 55
65
❹ 55
65
❹ 55
65
❹ 55
65

❹
55
65
❹ 55
❹ 65
❹ 55
❹ 65
❹ 55
65
❹ 55
65
55
65
55
65
55
65
65
55

Key

★ No mistakes
■ 1 mistake
⬭ 2 mistakes
▲ 3 mistakes
⬡ 4 mistakes

Music, Music, Music

Plotting a Picture

Music, Music, Music

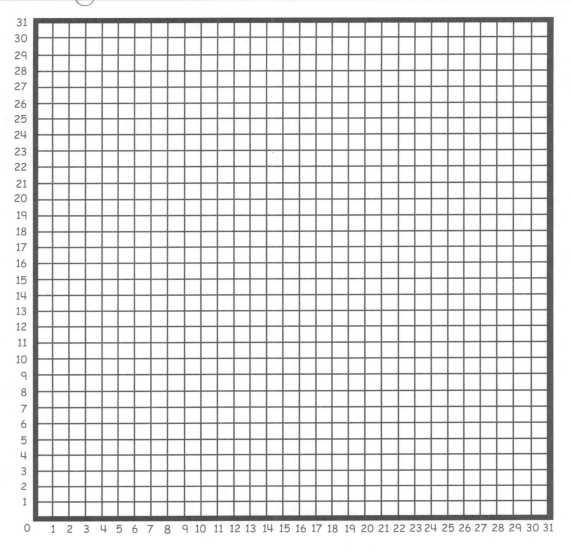

Plot the ordered pairs of numbers on the graph in the order in which they are listed, connecting them with straight lines. Start each new set of points with a new line.

▶ (14, 26) (14, 11) (13, 11) (11, 9) (10, 7) (10, 4)
(11, 2) (13, 0) (18, 0) (20, 2) (21, 4) (21, 7)
(20, 9) (18, 11) (17, 11) (17, 26) line ends

▶ (17, 27) (18, 27) (18, 26) (16, 26) (16, 27)
(17, 27) (17, 28) (18, 28) (18, 29) (16, 29)
(16, 28) (17, 28) line ends

▶ (14, 27) (15, 27) (15, 26) (13, 26) (13, 27)
(14, 27) (14, 28) (15, 28) (15, 29) (13, 29)
(13, 28) (14, 28) line ends

▶ (14, 29) (14, 30) (17, 30) (17, 29)
line ends

▶ (15, 29) (15, 2) line ends

▶ (16, 29) (16, 2) line ends

▶ (16, 3) (17, 4) (17, 5) (16, 6) (15, 6)
(14, 5) (14, 4) (15, 3) (16, 3)
line ends

Every band has at least one of these.

Skills:

Factors

Factors are all the numbers that divide evenly into a given number. For example, the factors of 15 are 1, 3, 5, and 15 because all of those numbers divide evenly into 15.

What are all the factors of the following numbers?

8

12

16

18

20

25

30

40

Music, Music, Music

Put It in Order

Skills:

Computation—
All Operations

Solve these problems.

(E) $\begin{array}{r} 5 \\ \times\ 4 \\ \hline \end{array}$ (S) $\begin{array}{r} 6 \\ \times\ 6 \\ \hline \end{array}$ (E) $\begin{array}{r} 12 \\ -\ 9 \\ \hline \end{array}$ (E) $\begin{array}{r} 10 \\ +\ 5 \\ \hline \end{array}$ (P) $\begin{array}{r} 27 \\ +13 \\ \hline \end{array}$ (T) $9 \div 9$ (A) $\begin{array}{r} 49 \\ -10 \\ \hline \end{array}$ (C) $\begin{array}{r} 6 \\ \times\ 5 \\ \hline \end{array}$

(R) $\begin{array}{r} 6 \\ +\ 5 \\ \hline \end{array}$ (E) $\begin{array}{r} 75 \\ -15 \\ \hline \end{array}$ (N) $\begin{array}{r} 10 \\ \times\ 5 \\ \hline \end{array}$ (U) $12 \div 2$ (E) $\begin{array}{r} 4 \\ \times\ 7 \\ \hline \end{array}$ (B) $\begin{array}{r} 39 \\ -20 \\ \hline \end{array}$ (M) $\begin{array}{r} 39 \\ +\ 4 \\ \hline \end{array}$ (S) $\begin{array}{r} 11 \\ \times\ 2 \\ \hline \end{array}$

(N) $\begin{array}{r} 14 \\ +11 \\ \hline \end{array}$ (M) $\begin{array}{r} 2 \\ \times\ 9 \\ \hline \end{array}$ (T) $\begin{array}{r} 20 \\ +\ 6 \\ \hline \end{array}$ (R) $\begin{array}{r} 45 \\ -11 \\ \hline \end{array}$ (U) $\begin{array}{r} 14 \\ +39 \\ \hline \end{array}$ (U) $\begin{array}{r} 5 \\ \times\ 7 \\ \hline \end{array}$ (N) $35 \div 7$ (M) $\begin{array}{r} 11 \\ \times\ 5 \\ \hline \end{array}$

(O) $\begin{array}{r} 11 \\ \times\ 3 \\ \hline \end{array}$ (R) $\begin{array}{r} 8 \\ \times\ 8 \\ \hline \end{array}$ (H) $\begin{array}{r} 59 \\ -28 \\ \hline \end{array}$ (M) $\begin{array}{r} 14 \\ +\ 0 \\ \hline \end{array}$ (E) $36 \div 4$ (O) $\begin{array}{r} 3 \\ \times\ 4 \\ \hline \end{array}$ (F) $\begin{array}{r} 31 \\ -18 \\ \hline \end{array}$ (S) $\begin{array}{r} 23 \\ +15 \\ \hline \end{array}$

(R) $\begin{array}{r} 46 \\ -\ 5 \\ \hline \end{array}$ (H) $\begin{array}{r} 9 \\ \times\ 3 \\ \hline \end{array}$ (I) $\begin{array}{r} 53 \\ -16 \\ \hline \end{array}$ (M) $28 \div 4$ (E) $\begin{array}{r} 5 \\ \times\ 9 \\ \hline \end{array}$ (I) $\begin{array}{r} 52 \\ -29 \\ \hline \end{array}$ (I) $\begin{array}{r} 7 \\ \times\ 6 \\ \hline \end{array}$ (B) $64 \div 8$

(B) $\begin{array}{r} 8 \\ \times\ 7 \\ \hline \end{array}$ (R) $\begin{array}{r} 35 \\ -14 \\ \hline \end{array}$ (H) $16 \div 8$

Write the answers in order from smallest to largest. Then write the letter for each answer on the following lines.

smallest

___ ___ ___ ___   ___ ___ ___ ___ ___ ___ ___ ___ ___   ___ ___ ___

___ ___ ___ ___ ___ ___ ___ ___ ___ ___   ___ ___

___ ___ ___ ___ ___ ___ ___ ___ ___ ___ ___ ___

___ ___ ___ ___ ___ ___ ___ ___   ___ ___ ___ ___ ___

largest

TEST YOUR SKILLS

Solve these problems. Fill in the circle to show the correct answer.

$159 49 + 36	$22.50 − 19.95	$229 x 2	$37.75 + 14.25	$110 x 5
Ⓐ $144	Ⓐ $1.45	Ⓐ $227	Ⓐ $52.00	Ⓐ $555
Ⓑ $254	Ⓑ $10.55	Ⓑ $458	Ⓑ $23.50	Ⓑ $550
Ⓒ $244	Ⓒ $2.45	Ⓒ $231	Ⓒ $41.90	Ⓒ $500
Ⓓ $248	Ⓓ $2.55	Ⓓ $598	Ⓓ $51.50	Ⓓ $560

Write all of the factors of 20.

Match.

fifteen	2,987
twenty-seven	15
two thousand nine hundred eighty-seven	8,800
five thousand sixteen	27
ninety-four	94
eight thousand eight hundred	5,016

Fill in the circle for the correct time.

When is 4 hours after 7:00 a.m.?	When is 15 minutes after 4:30 p.m.?	When is 25 minutes after 4:15 p.m.?
Ⓐ 3:00 a.m. Ⓒ 10:00 a.m.	Ⓐ 4:45 p.m. Ⓒ 5:15 p.m.	Ⓐ 4:10 p.m. Ⓒ 4:40 p.m.
Ⓑ 11:00 p.m. Ⓓ 11:00 a.m.	Ⓑ 4:45 a.m. Ⓓ 4:15 p.m.	Ⓑ 4:30 p.m. Ⓓ 4:40 a.m.
When is 2 hours before 9:00 a.m.?	When is 2 hours after 1:00 a.m.?	When is 10 minutes before 12 noon?
Ⓐ 11:00 p.m. Ⓒ 7:00 p.m.	Ⓐ 3:00 p.m. Ⓒ 3:00 a.m.	Ⓐ 12:10 p.m. Ⓒ 11:50 a.m.
Ⓑ 7:00 a.m. Ⓓ 11:00 a.m.	Ⓑ 11:00 a.m. Ⓓ 11:00 p.m.	Ⓑ 2:00 a.m. Ⓓ 11:50 p.m.

Count the cubes.

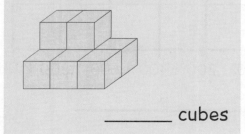

_____ cubes

Plot the ordered pairs of numbers.

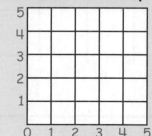

(1, 2) (1, 5) (4, 5) (4, 2) (1, 2)

Circle the shape you made.

School Candy Sale

1 The school has been selling candy bars to raise money for a new playground. There are 20 classrooms in the school, and each classroom made an average of $300 in profit. What is the total amount of profit that the school made?

$ _____ total profit

3 The following table shows the number of each item that was sold by the school. How many total items were sold?

almond bars	2,000
mints	1,380
caramels	1,560
peanut butter cups	1,220
toffee bars	1,400
almond clusters	1,980

_____ items total

2 The almond bars were shipped to the school in cases. Each case had 10 boxes with 25 candy bars in each box. How many cases of almond bars were sent to the school to supply the order of 2,000 almond bars?

_____ cases of almond bars

Complete the bar graph to show the number of candy bars sold. Label each axis.

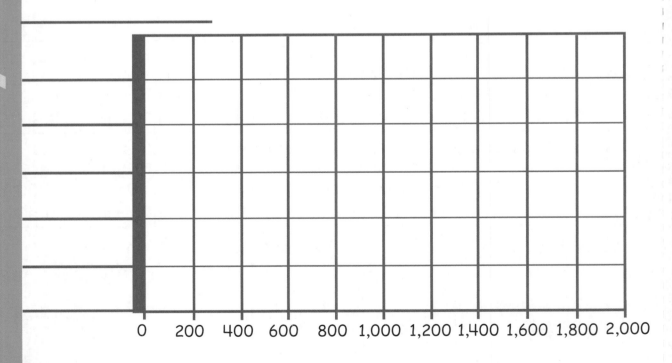

0   200   400   600   800   1,000 1,200 1,400 1,600 1,800 2,000

Skills:

Computation—
All Operations

Solve the following problems to find a clue about how much each type of candy costs. After solving each problem, look at the key at the bottom of the page to see which letter corresponds to the answer. Write the letter on the line below each problem.

$\begin{array}{r}9\\ \times 2\\ \hline 18\end{array}$ $\begin{array}{r}5\\ \times 1\\ \hline \end{array}$ $21 \div 7$ $\begin{array}{r}1\\ \times 5\\ \hline \end{array}$ $\begin{array}{r}8\\ + 2\\ \hline \end{array}$ $9 \div 9$ $\begin{array}{r}46\\ - 39\\ \hline \end{array}$ $\begin{array}{r}1\\ \times 2\\ \hline \end{array}$

C ___ ___ ___ ___ ___ ___ ___

$\begin{array}{r}29\\ - 11\\ \hline \end{array}$ $\begin{array}{r}7\\ \times 3\\ \hline \end{array}$ $12 \div 6$ $\begin{array}{r}72\\ - 56\\ \hline \end{array}$ $63 \div 7$ $\begin{array}{r}65\\ - 44\\ \hline \end{array}$ $\begin{array}{r}15\\ + 12\\ \hline \end{array}$ $12 \div 4$

___ ___ ___ ___   ___ ___ ___ ___

$\begin{array}{r}2\\ \times 3\\ \hline \end{array}$ $\begin{array}{r}16\\ + 5\\ \hline \end{array}$ $\begin{array}{r}1\\ + 6\\ \hline \end{array}$ $\begin{array}{r}5\\ + 2\\ \hline \end{array}$ $45 \div 9$ $18 \div 6$ $14 \div 7$ $\begin{array}{r}15\\ + 0\\ \hline \end{array}$ $8 \div 8$ $\begin{array}{r}46\\ - 43\\ \hline \end{array}$

___ ___ ___ ___ ___ ___ ___   ___ ___ ___

$\begin{array}{r}27\\ + 3\\ \hline \end{array}$ $\begin{array}{r}7\\ \times 3\\ \hline \end{array}$ $\begin{array}{r}7\\ \times 8\\ \hline \end{array}$

___ ___ ___

Key

1 = E	2 = S	3 = R	5 = A	6 = D
7 = L	9 = F	10 = M	15 = P	16 = T
18 = C	21 = O	27 = U	30 = B	56 = X

The Candy Sale

Managing Multiples

Multiples are the product of a whole number and any other given number. For example, the first five multiples of 7 are 7, 14, 21, 28, and 35. These numbers come from the following products:

$$7 \times 1 = 7 \qquad 7 \times 4 = 28$$
$$7 \times 2 = 14 \qquad 7 \times 5 = 35$$
$$7 \times 3 = 21$$

What are the first five multiples for each of the following numbers?

4

9

3

8

6

2

5

10

The Candy Sale

Skills:

Computation—
Addition,
Subtraction,
Multiplication

Use the digits 0 through 9 to complete these number sentences. Use each number only once. Is there more than one possible solution? _____

0 1 2 3 4 5 6 7 8 9

$1\boxed{} + \boxed{}4 = 43$

$$\begin{array}{r} \boxed{} \\ \times\ 8 \\ \hline 2\boxed{} \end{array}$$

$$\begin{array}{r} \boxed{} \\ \times\ 7 \\ \hline \boxed{}\,\boxed{} \end{array}$$

$$\begin{array}{r} 4\,\boxed{} \\ -\ \boxed{}\,3 \\ \hline 2\,\boxed{} \end{array}$$

©2005 by Evan-Moor Corp. • EMC 4548 • Math

The Candy Sale

UNIT 4   **43**

Tongue Twister

Find the area of each figure. Then write the corresponding letter on each line above the area. Read the tongue twister and try to say it quickly three times.

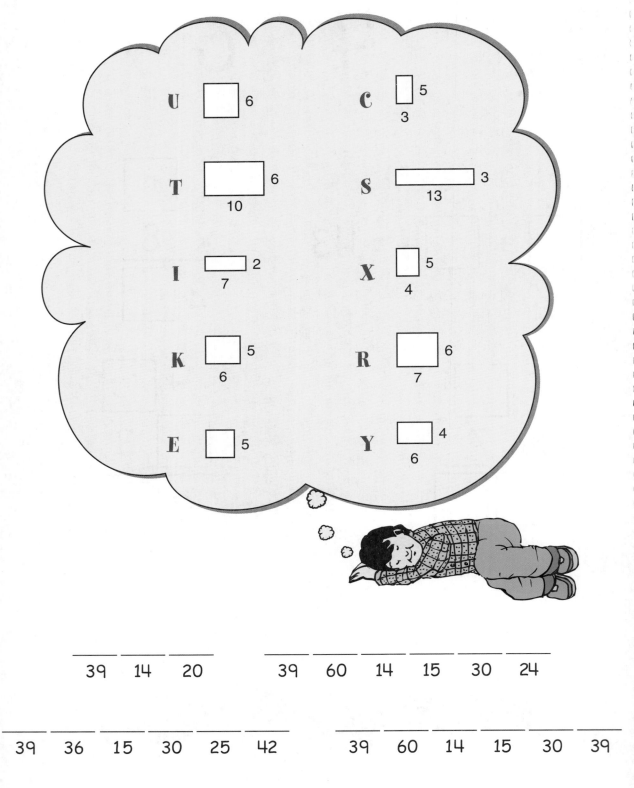

The Candy Sale

$\overline{}\ \overline{}\ \overline{}$
39 14 20

$\overline{}\ \overline{}\ \overline{}\ \overline{}\ \overline{}\ \overline{}$
39 60 14 15 30 24

$\overline{}\ \overline{}\ \overline{}\ \overline{}\ \overline{}\ \overline{}$
39 36 15 30 25 42

$\overline{}\ \overline{}\ \overline{}\ \overline{}\ \overline{}\ \overline{}$
39 60 14 15 30 39

Skills:

Fractions

The following pictures represent candy bars that have been partially eaten. Look at each candy bar and write the fraction that represents the remaining part.

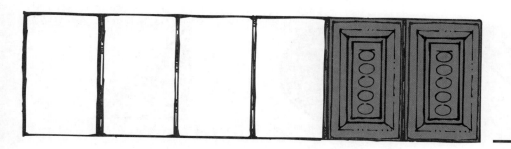

_____

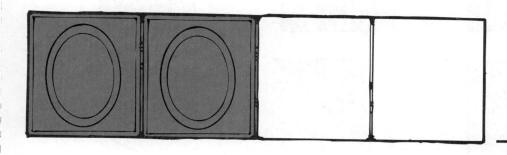

_____

_____

_____

The Candy Sale

Mystery Numbers

Each of the following shapes represents a number: 1, 2, 3, 4, 6, and 8. Use the equations to determine the value of each shape. The value of each shape is the same throughout the entire page. Write the values on the shapes at the bottom of the page.

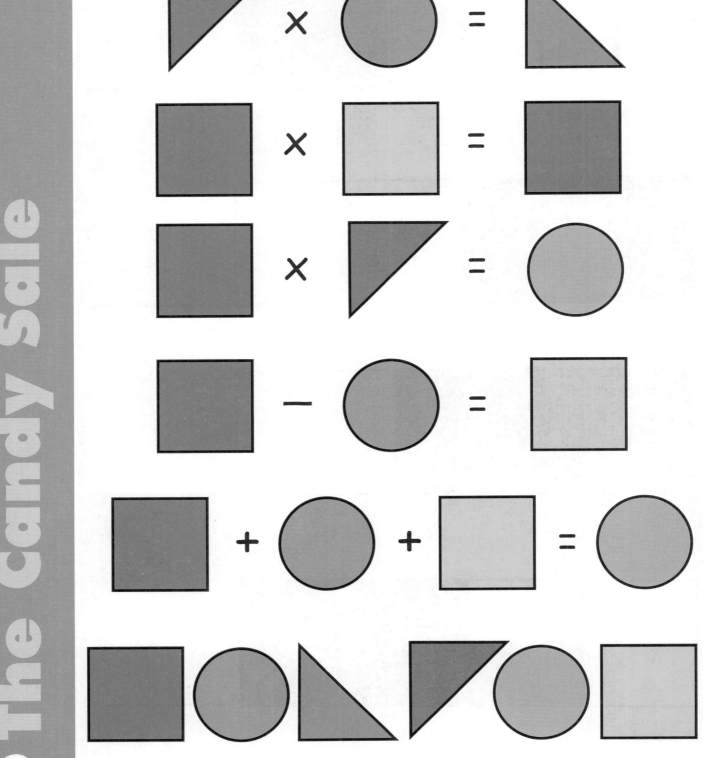

The Candy Sale

The toffee bars are shipped 48 bars in a shipping box. Each layer in the box has the same number of bars. How many bars would there be in each layer if there were

6 layers? _____

4 layers? _____

2 layers? _____

A case of mints has 72 boxes. Draw two different ways in which these boxes could be packed.

Draw one way that 24 boxes of almond clusters could be arranged in a shipping box.

The Candy Sale

How Much Does It Weigh?

If each toffee bar weighs 10 ounces,
how many ounces will an entire case
of 48 toffee bars weigh?

_____ ounces

One pound equals 16 ounces.
How many pounds will the
48 toffee bars weigh?

_____ pounds

If each box of mints weighs
8 ounces, how many ounces will
an entire case of 72 boxes
weigh?

_____ ounces

Boxes of almond clusters are
packed in cases of 24. If each box
of almond clusters weighs 2 pounds,
how many pounds will an entire case
weigh?

_____ pounds

The almond bars are shipped in
boxes of 30. If each box of almond
bars weighs $1\frac{1}{2}$ pounds, how many
pounds will an entire case weigh?

_____ pounds

The Candy Sale

Solve the following problems and match them up with the answers in the key. Write the answer letters in order of the problems to spell out the type of candy that sells for two dollars a box.

Key

6 = O	9 = R	10 = E	23 = A	25 = F
26 = E	35 = S	36 = T	45 = M	49 = B
56 = C	65 = F	66 = A	75 = S	81 = R

1. $12 \times 3 =$ _____

2. $25 - 19 =$ _____

3. $5 \times 5 =$ _____

4. $27 + 38 =$ _____

5. $30 \div 3 =$ _____

6. $17 + 9 =$ _____

7. $7 \times 7 =$ _____

8. $77 - 11 =$ _____

9. $27 \div 3 =$ _____

10. $7 \times 5 =$ _____

What candy sells for two dollars a box?

___ ___ ___ ___ ___   ___ ___ ___ ___

The Candy Sale

Complete the Orders

An order sheet for the candy sale is shown below. Complete the column that states the total amount due, and then determine the change that each person should get in return.

	$1	$2	$3	$4	$5	$6	Total Due
Jim Johnson	2	4	1	0	0	1	
Valerie Leal	1	0	2	2	1	0	
Vivian Vance	0	0	3	0	2	0	
Julio Martinez	2	0	6	2	0	0	
Nancy Pauls	3	0	1	0	0	0	
George Moreno	0	0	0	0	2	0	
Austin Phillips	1	3	0	0	0	1	
Regina Hernandez	5	0	0	0	0	0	
Annette Dolan	0	2	0	4	1	1	

	Amount Paid	Change
Jim Johnson	$20.00	
Valerie Leal	$20.00	
Vivian Vance	$20.00	
Julio Martinez	$40.00	
Nancy Pauls	$10.00	
George Moreno	$20.00	
Austin Phillips	$13.00	
Regina Hernandez	$10.00	
Annette Dolan	$40.00	

Math • EMC 4548 • ©2005 by Evan-Moor Corp.

Skills:

Logic

Complete this logic puzzle to determine how much each kind of candy costs. Use the clues on pages 41 and 49, as well as the clues at the bottom of this page.

	One Dollar	Two Dollars	Three Dollars	Four Dollars	Five Dollars	Six Dollars
Almond Bars						
Mints						
Caramels						
Peanut Butter Cups						
Toffee Bars						
Almond Clusters						

The Candy Sale

Clues

Each candy sells for a different price.

The almond bars cost more than the caramels.

The almond clusters cost more than the almond bars.

The mints are less than three dollars.

TEST YOUR
SKILLS

$$3 \times 4$$

$$6 \times 6$$

$$9 \times 8$$

$$5 \times 6$$

30 ÷ 5 = _____   28 ÷ 7 = _____   48 ÷ 8 = _____   24 ÷ 3 = _____

What is a good estimate for the length of a tape needed to record the following songs?

3 minutes	24 seconds
2 minutes	5 seconds
4 minutes	55 seconds
3 minutes	10 seconds
5 minutes	58 seconds

_____

Write the number three hundred seventy-five in numerical form.

_____

What are all the factors of 12?

_____

When is 3 hours and 10 minutes after 5:15 p.m.?

_____

When is 5 hours and 40 minutes before 2:00 a.m.?

_____

What are the first four multiples of 5?

_____

How many blocks are in this figure?

_____

Skills:
Computation—
All Operations

During winter vacation from school, six families went on trips to different locations. Solve the following problems to get a clue about where one family went during the winter break. After solving each problem, look at the key at the bottom of the page to see what letter corresponds to the answer, and then write it on the line below the problem.

$$\begin{array}{r} 15 \\ +\ 8 \\ \hline 23 \end{array} \qquad \begin{array}{r} 4 \\ \times\ 7 \\ \hline \end{array} \qquad 25 \div 5 \qquad\qquad \begin{array}{r} 8 \\ +32 \\ \hline \end{array} \qquad 90 \div 9 \qquad \begin{array}{r} 74 \\ -39 \\ \hline \end{array} \qquad \begin{array}{r} 1 \\ \times\ 5 \\ \hline \end{array}$$

_T_ __ __   __ __ __ __

$$\begin{array}{r} 50 \\ -11 \\ \hline \end{array} \quad 27 \div 9 \quad \begin{array}{r} 5 \\ \times\ 6 \\ \hline \end{array} \quad \begin{array}{r} 66 \\ -56 \\ \hline \end{array} \quad \begin{array}{r} 8 \\ \times\ 7 \\ \hline \end{array} \quad \begin{array}{r} 61 \\ -44 \\ \hline \end{array} \qquad \begin{array}{r} 0 \\ +12 \\ \hline \end{array} \quad 30 \div 6 \quad \begin{array}{r} 8 \\ \times\ 2 \\ \hline \end{array} \quad \begin{array}{r} 17 \\ +\ 6 \\ \hline \end{array}$$

__ __ __ __ __ __   __ __ __ __

$$\begin{array}{r} 23 \\ +\ 9 \\ \hline \end{array} \quad \begin{array}{r} 10 \\ +\ 5 \\ \hline \end{array} \quad \begin{array}{r} 5 \\ \times\ 2 \\ \hline \end{array} \quad 20 \div 2 \quad \begin{array}{r} 4 \\ \times\ 4 \\ \hline \end{array} \quad \begin{array}{r} 8 \\ \times\ 6 \\ \hline \end{array}$$

__ __ __ __ __ __

Key

3 = A	5 = E	10 = I	12 = W	15 = K
16 = N	17 = Y	23 = T	28 = H	30 = M
32 = S	35 = C	39 = F	40 = R	48 = G
56 = L				

Winter Break

Estimating

For each of the following questions, circle the best **estimate**.

About how long is a car from the front bumper to the back bumper?

    a. 20 meters

    b. 5 meters

    c. 2 meters

About how tall is a book?

    a. 3 meters

    b. 3 centimeters

    c. 30 centimeters

About how tall is a door?

    a. 7 feet

    b. 7 inches

    c. 7 yards

About how long is a new pencil?

    a. 8 inches

    b. 8 centimeters

    c. 8 feet

About how tall is a 12-year-old boy?

    a. 3 meters

    b. 30 inches

    c. 5 feet

About how long does a CD play if it plays all the songs?

    a. 15 minutes

    b. 50 minutes

    c. 3 hours

About how long does it take you to brush your teeth in the morning?

    a. 20 minutes

    b. 1 hour

    c. 3 minutes

About how long does it take you to walk up 12 steps?

    a. 15 seconds

    b. 5 minutes

    c. one-half hour

Hidden in the numbers below are at least 25 sets of numbers that can be written as a multiplication or division problem. The equations may read forward (left to right), down, or diagonally. Circle as many problems as you can find.

3	20	38	36	9	4	1	5	3	9	9	5
1	8	4	6	10	8	4	5	17	28	4	3
23	17	24	16	7	19	7	25	7	4	28	36
8	6	15	64	8	8	27	56	3	31	7	6
6	7	4	7	7	2	14	5	4	4	24	3
48	7	3	21	6	6	9	29	12	9	8	72
17	40	39	3	5	4	42	5	13	11	16	18
9	6	54	27	41	21	17	6	45	81	4	3
16	12	6	9	4	8	32	8	7	29	9	6
1	5	7	3	9	10	5	2	7	8	24	9
3	13	6	18	3	20	7	1	49	16	5	7
2	8	16	30	3	24	6	4	5	3	15	34

The circled equation reads: $3 \times 8 = 24$

Winter Fun

Plot the ordered pairs of numbers on the graph in the order in which they are listed. Start each new set of points with a new line.

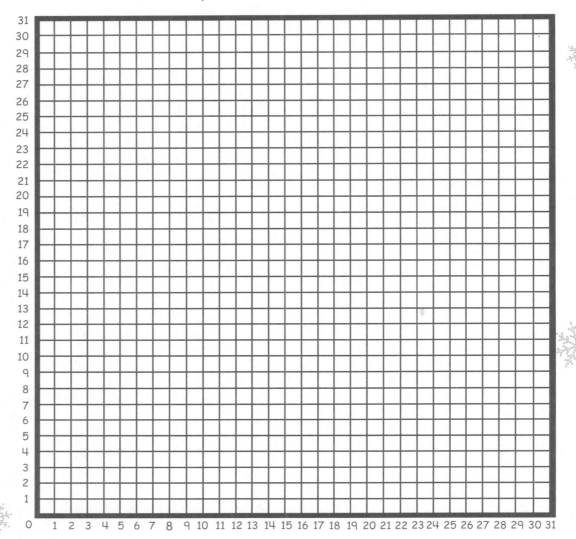

► (15, 4) (16, 4) (16, 12) (15, 3) (17, 3)
(17, 2) (26, 2) (27, 3) (27, 2) (26, 1)
(3, 1) (3, 2) (14, 2) (14, 22) (15, 23)
(15, 24) (14, 25) (14, 27) (15, 28)
(16, 28) (17, 27) (17, 25) (16, 24)
(16, 23) (17, 23) (18, 22) (24, 18)
(24, 17) (18, 21) (18, 20) line ends

► (18, 18) (18, 13) (17, 5) (19, 5) (19, 4)
(28, 4) (29, 5) (29, 4) (28, 3) (17, 3)
line ends

► (14, 3) (5, 3) (5, 4) (14, 4) line ends

► (15, 21) (21, 15) (21, 16) (17, 21) line ends

► (21, 15) (21, 4) line ends

► (24, 17) (24, 5) line ends

► (20, 5) (22, 5) line ends

► (23, 6) (25, 6) line ends

The drawing shows one kind of winter fun.

The family that went to Disneyland had the following events happen throughout the day. Read the clocks and identify the time each event occurred.

They arrived
at the park at _____ :_____ .

They had lunch at _____ :_____ .

Little brother
tripped and fell at _____ :_____ .

They bought fruit
for a snack at _____ :_____ .

They saw the
pirate show at _____ :_____ .

They left Disneyland to
return to the hotel at _____ :_____ .

A-Maze-ing!

One family walked through a gigantic maze.

At each question mark, circle the larger number. Then follow the path with the larger number through the maze.

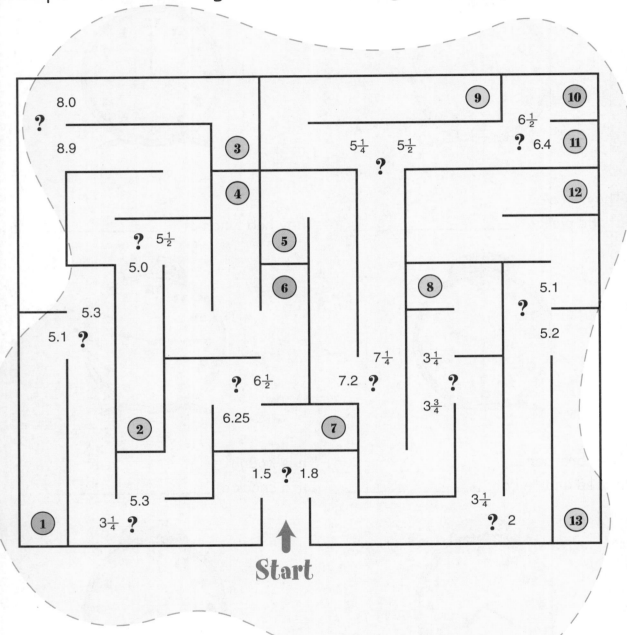

What number was at the end of the path? _____

Skills:

Patterning—
Figures and
Numbers

Write or draw the three numbers or figures that would come next in each of the following patterns.

1   3   5   7   9   11   13   _____ _____ _____

_____ _____ _____

_____ _____ _____

3   6   9   12   15   _____ _____ _____

_____ _____ _____

B   E   H   K   N   _____ _____ _____

5   9   13   17   21   _____ _____ _____

_____ _____ _____

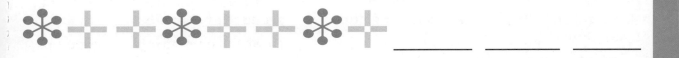

_____ _____ _____

8   14   17   23   26   32   35   _____ _____ _____

Winter Break

Using a Floor Plan

The map below shows the floor plan of the hotel where one of the families stayed. It shows 8 rooms lettered A through H. The red doors connect the rooms. The maids have a certain path that they use to clean the rooms. However, today they kept leaving items in rooms and had to go through the rooms in an unusual order. Starting in Room A, answer the questions below to determine the order in which they went through the rooms. If you get to a room without the correct answer, then backtrack to see if you made a mistake.

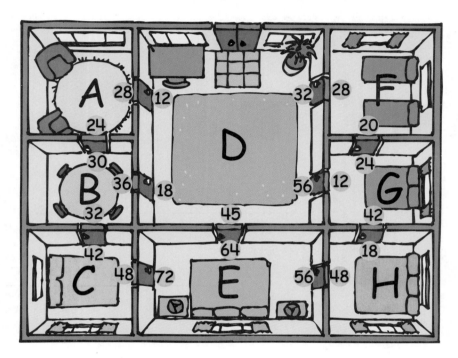

1. The maids started in Room A. Go through the doorway that is the product of 6 and 4.

   What room are you in now? _____

2. Go through the doorway that is the difference of 40 and 8.

   What room are you in now? _____

3. Go through the doorway with the product of 7 and 6.

   What room are you in now? _____

4. Go through the doorway with the sum of 18 and 18.

   What room are you in now? _____

5. Go through the doorway with the product of 5 and 9.

   What room are you in now? _____

6. Go through the doorway with the sum of 25 and 31.

   What room are you in now? _____

7. Go through the doorway with the product of 6 and 3.

   What room are you in now? _____

8. Go through the doorway with the difference of 20 and 8.

   What room are you in now? _____

9. Go through the doorway with the product of 4 and 8.

   In what room have you ended up?

   _____

Skills:

Number Words

Draw a straight line to connect each numerical form with its corresponding word form.

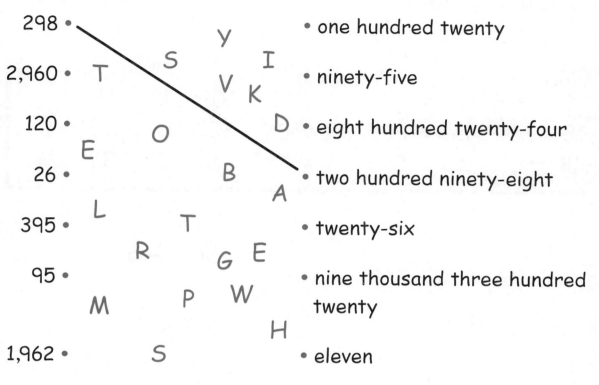

298 •

2,960 •

120 •

26 •

395 •

95 •

1,962 •

824 •

11 •

9,320 •

• one hundred twenty

• ninety-five

• eight hundred twenty-four

• two hundred ninety-eight

• twenty-six

• nine thousand three hundred twenty

• eleven

• three hundred ninety-five

• two thousand nine hundred sixty

• one thousand nine hundred sixty-two

Write the letters that are inside each closed figure. These letters can be arranged to spell the name of the family that stayed home during the winter break.

Which family stayed home?

HINT:
A closed figure is a polygon with straight lines on all sides without any "invisible" sides to the shape.

Winter Break

Find the Answer

Skills:

Computation—
All Operations

Solve the following problems and match them up with the answers in the key. Write the answer letters in the order of the problems to spell out where the Jordan family went during their winter break.

Key

6 = E	7 = X	9 = N	10 = I	13 = N
18 = A	24 = H	28 = D	32 = D	35 = S
48 = L	56 = O	63 = Y	75 = C	81 = M

1. $8 \times 4 =$ _____

2. $29 - 19 =$ _____

3. $7 \times 5 =$ _____

4. $47 - 34 =$ _____

5. $30 \div 5 =$ _____

6. $17 + 46 =$ _____

7. $8 \times 6 =$ _____

8. $37 - 19 =$ _____

9. $27 \div 3 =$ _____

10. $7 \times 4 =$ _____

Where did the Jordan family go during winter break?

___ ___ ___ ___ ___ ___ ___ ___ ___ ___

Use this map to answer the questions.

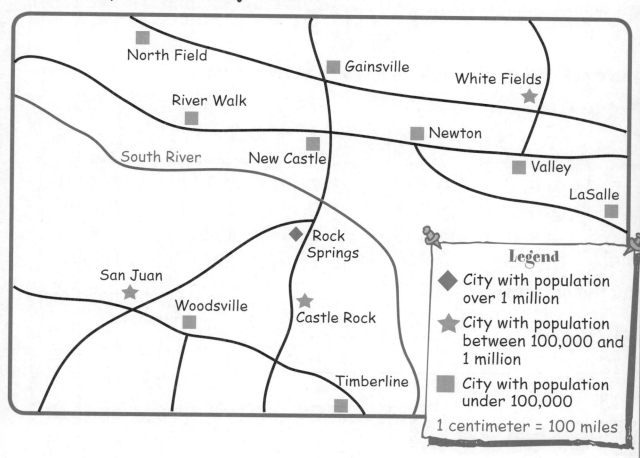

How many cities have a population between 100,000 and 1,000,000? _____

In this legend, 1 centimeter = 100 miles. Use this key and a centimeter ruler to estimate the following distances in miles.

About how far apart are North Field and River Walk? _____

About how many miles is it between San Juan and Newton? _____

About how far is it from White Fields to Timberline? _____

About how many miles is it between Woodsville and White Fields? _____

About how far is it from LaSalle to Gainsville? _____

Winter Break

TEST YOUR SKILLS

Read the clock. Fill in the circle to show the correct time.

Ⓐ 2:55	Ⓐ 9:15	Ⓐ 6:10	Ⓐ 7:40	Ⓐ 4:30	Ⓐ 3:40
Ⓑ 2:00	Ⓑ 3:45	Ⓑ 2:25	Ⓑ 8:35	Ⓑ 6:15	Ⓑ 8:15
Ⓒ 11:05	Ⓒ 9:20	Ⓒ 6:15	Ⓒ 7:35	Ⓒ 6:20	Ⓒ 8:45
Ⓓ 11:10	Ⓓ 4:15	Ⓓ 2:30	Ⓓ 7:45	Ⓓ 4:35	Ⓓ 3:45

Continue the pattern.

7   10   13   ____ ____ ____

6   12   18   ____ ____ ____

7   13   9   15   ____ ____

⬤ ◼ ⬤ ⬤ ◼ ◼   ____ ____ ____

Circle the larger numbers.

8.0   or   8.9

$5\frac{1}{4}$ or $5\frac{1}{2}$

$6\frac{1}{2}$ or   6.4

$7\frac{1}{2}$ or   7.25

Use the centimeter ruler to answer these questions about line length.

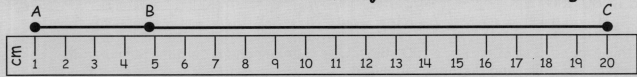

About how far is it from point A to point C? _____ cm

About how far is it from point A to point B? _____ cm

How much farther from point A is point C than point B? _____ cm

Fill in the circle for the best estimate.

About how long is a car from the front bumper to the rear bumper?
   Ⓐ 20 meters   Ⓑ 5 meters   Ⓒ 2 meters   Ⓓ 10 centimeters

About how tall is a cat?
   Ⓐ 2 meters   Ⓑ 2 centimeters   Ⓒ 2 feet   Ⓓ 20 centimeters

About how long is a new pencil?
   Ⓐ 8 inches   Ⓑ 8 centimeters   Ⓒ 4 feet   Ⓓ 4 centimeters

Six children each have a different pet. Solve the following problems and find the first clue to help determine which pet is owned by each person. After solving each problem, look at the key at the bottom of the page to see which letter corresponds to the answer, and then write it on the line below each problem.

$$\begin{array}{r} 15 \\ +20 \\ \hline 35 \end{array} \qquad \begin{array}{r} 3 \\ \times 3 \\ \hline \end{array} \qquad 15 \div 5 \qquad \begin{array}{r} 7 \\ \times 6 \\ \hline \end{array} \qquad \begin{array}{r} 5 \\ \times 5 \\ \hline \end{array} \qquad 45 \div 9 \qquad \begin{array}{r} 3 \\ \times 2 \\ \hline \end{array} \qquad \begin{array}{r} 9 \\ \times 7 \\ \hline \end{array}$$

J __ __ __ __   __ __ __ __

$$\begin{array}{r} 50 \\ -\ 8 \\ \hline \end{array} \qquad 35 \div 7 \qquad \begin{array}{r} 9 \\ \times 8 \\ \hline \end{array} \qquad \begin{array}{r} 66 \\ -61 \\ \hline \end{array} \qquad \begin{array}{r} 12 \\ +\ 7 \\ \hline \end{array} \qquad \begin{array}{r} 61 \\ -19 \\ \hline \end{array} \qquad \begin{array}{r} 60 \\ +12 \\ \hline \end{array} \qquad \begin{array}{r} 8 \\ \times 3 \\ \hline \end{array} \qquad 36 \div 6$$

__ __ __   __ __ __   __ __ __

$$\begin{array}{r} 23 \\ +\ 2 \\ \hline \end{array} \qquad \begin{array}{r} 0 \\ +5 \\ \hline \end{array} \qquad \begin{array}{r} 6 \\ \times 3 \\ \hline \end{array}$$

__ __ __

Key

3 = A	5 = O	6 = E	9 = U
18 = G	19 = W	24 = H	25 = D
3_	42 = N	63 = S	72 = T

Name the Pet

Use the number 9,369,639,201 for the following problems. Each of the numbers on the left has been rounded off to a different place value. Draw a straight line connecting the number to the place value that it has been rounded off to.

9,000,000,000

9,369,639,200

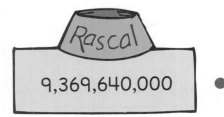

9,369,640,000

9,369,600,000

9,400,000,000

9,370,000,000

● Ten-millions

● Hundred-thousands

● Hundred-millions

● Billions

● Ten-thousands

● T

MC 4548 • ©2005 by

Math • F   Corp.

Pet Pals

What Kind of Suit Does Jake's Pet Duck Wear?

To solve the riddle, draw a line connecting the figure on the left with the number of lines of symmetry it has on the right. Write the letter that the line passes through in front of the figure. Read the answer from top to bottom.

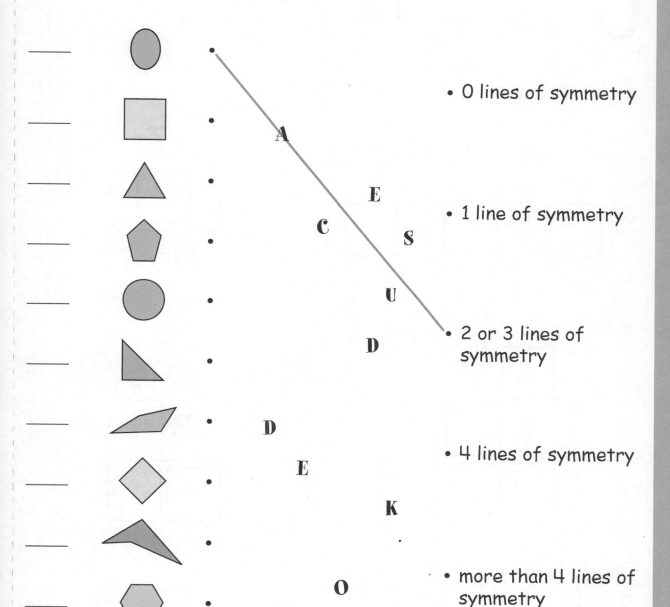

• 0 lines of symmetry

A

E

C

S

• 1 line of symmetry

U

D

• 2 or 3 lines of symmetry

D

• 4 lines of symmetry

E

K

O

• more than 4 lines of symmetry

Number Square Puzzler

Use the digits 0 through 9 to complete these number sentences. Use each number only once. Is there more than one possible solution? _____

0 1 2 3 4 5 6 7 8 9

$$2\Box \div \Box = \Box$$

$$\begin{array}{r} 7 \\ \times\ \Box \\ \hline 56 \end{array}$$

$$\begin{array}{r} \Box\ 7 \\ -\ 1\ \Box \\ \hline \Box\ 1 \end{array}$$

$$\begin{array}{r} 1\ 6 \\ +\ 3\ \Box \\ \hline \Box\ \Box \end{array}$$

Math • EMC 4548 • ©2005 by Evan-Moor Corp.

Skills:
Computation—
All Operations

Beginning at Start, follow the red arrows through the circles of problems, doing each problem. Use the answer from the previous problem to complete the next problem. What is the final answer in the yellow circle?

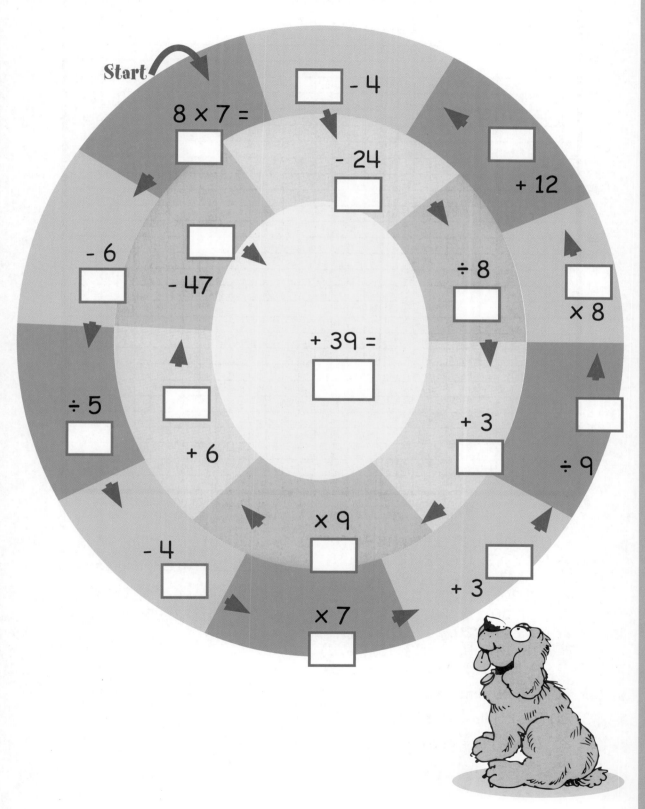

Pet Pals

A Purr-fect Pet

Plot the ordered pairs of numbers on the graph in the order in which they are listed, connecting them with straight lines. Start each new set of points with a new line.

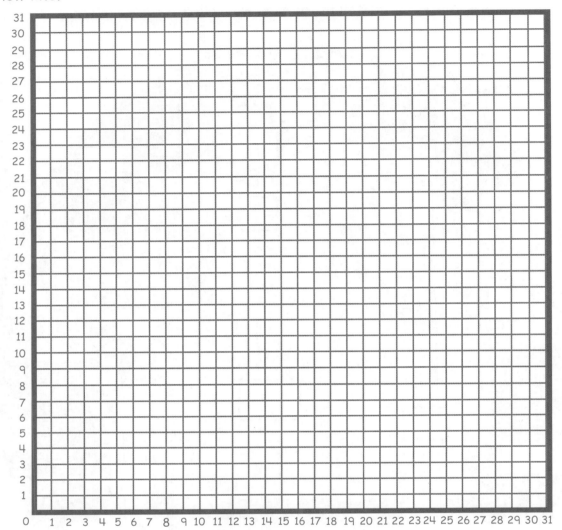

► (12, 9) (13, 9) (15, 8) (17, 6) (18, 4) (18, 2)
(22, 2) (21, 1) (3, 1) (2, 2) (2, 7) (4, 9)
(5, 8) (3, 6) (3, 3) (4, 2) (10, 2) (9, 4)
(9, 12) (13, 20) (13, 22) (11, 24) (11, 26)
(13, 28) (14, 30) (15, 28) (16, 28) (17, 30)
(18, 28) (20, 26) (20, 24) (18, 22) (17, 21)
(17, 20) (18, 19) (19, 17) (19, 15) (24, 1)
(23, 1) (19, 12) (19, 9) (18, 4) line ends

► (13, 20) (17, 20) line ends

► (13, 21) (17, 21) line ends

► (12, 25) (9, 24) line ends

► (12, 25) (9, 25) line ends

► (12, 26) (9, 26) line ends

► (12, 26) (9, 27) line ends

► (19, 25) (22, 24) line ends

► (19, 25) (22, 25) line ends

► (19, 26) (22, 26) line ends

► (19, 26) (22, 27) line ends

► (14, 26) (14, 27) (15, 27) (15, 26)
(14, 26) line ends

► (16, 26) (16, 27) (17, 27) (17, 26)
(16, 26) line ends

► (15, 23) (15, 24) (16, 24) (16, 23)
(15, 23) line ends

Skills:
Computation—
All Operations

Solve the following problems and match them up with the answers in the key. The letters, in the order of the problems, spell out one of the pets.

Key

1 = R	2 = B	3 = O	4 = A	5 = I
6 = O	16 = O	18 = O	20 = S	24 = N
25 = F	26 = C	28 = M	30 = T	48 = R
49 = F	56 = S	64 = C	70 = T	81 = P

1. $8 \div 4 =$ _____

2. $6 \times 3 =$ _____

3. $24 \div 6 =$ _____

4. $14 + 12 =$ _____

5. $4 \times 4 =$ _____

6. $8 \times 3 =$ _____

7. $2 + 18 =$ _____

8. $57 - 27 =$ _____

9. $6 \times 8 =$ _____

10. $35 \div 7 =$ _____

11. $8 \times 8 =$ _____

12. $53 + 17 =$ _____

13. $21 - 18 =$ _____

14. $7 \div 7 =$ _____

What is the pet?

___ ___ ___

___ ___ ___ ___ ___ ___ ___ ___ ___ ___ ___

Pet Pals

At the Pet Store

Solve these problems.

When one pet owner went to the pet store to buy pet food, the person brought a $5 bill. The food cost $2.97 including tax. How much change was given back?

$ _____

Another pet owner wants to buy a leash, a collar, and a new water dish for the dog. The leash sells for $3.99. The collar sells for $4.55. The water dish sells for $5.99. If the owner has $14.50, will that be enough to buy the items? Why or why not?

The turtle's owner is buying a new aquarium for the turtle. The store will give the owner $10.00 for the old aquarium, and the new aquarium costs $29.90 including tax. If the owner gives the pet store a $20.00 bill, what change will be given back?

$ _____

The pet owner who had the fish went to the pet store to buy another fish. The fish cost 79¢. Name three different combinations of coins that would add up to exactly 79¢.

Carolina walked the dog and two other dogs around the block. The other two dogs' owners each paid her $2.00 to walk their dogs. If this happened every day for two weeks, how much money would she make?

$ _____

Pet Pals

Use an inch ruler to complete these measurements. What is the length of each animal to the nearest $\frac{1}{4}$ inch?

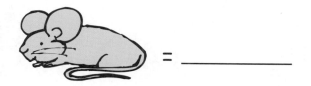 = _____

 = _____

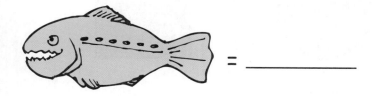 = _____

 = _____

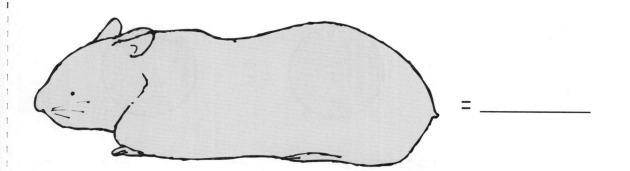 = _____

 = _____

Pet Pals

Mystery Numbers

Each of the following shapes represents a different number: 1, 2, 3, 5, 6, and 9. Use the equations to determine the value of each shape. The value of each shape is the same throughout the entire page. Write the values on the shapes at the bottom of the page.

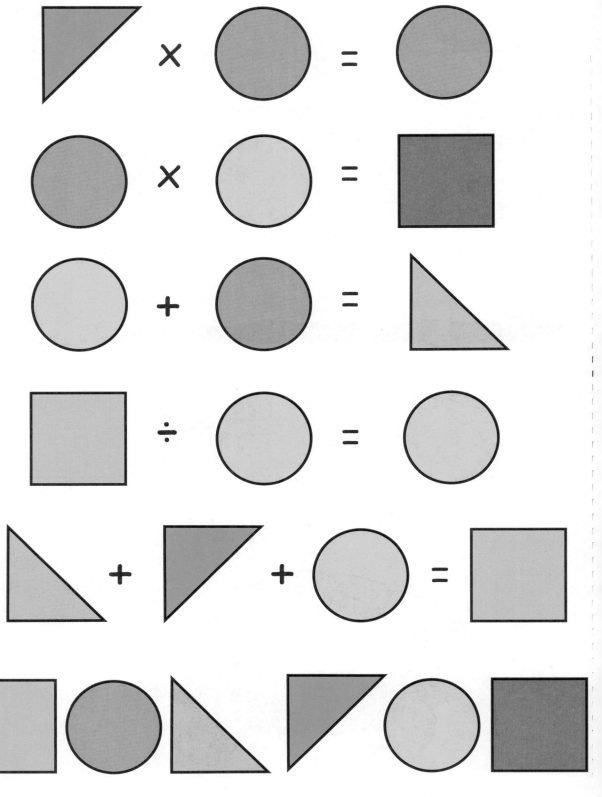

Math • EMC 4548 • ©2005 by Evan-Moor Corp.

Skills:

Ordinal
Numbers

Six children brought their pets to school to show their class. Use the following clues to determine in what order they showed their pets.

Clues

The snake was after the turtle and before the cat.

The fish was not last.

The dog was next to the rabbit but not next to the turtle.

The owner of the rabbit got to show it first.

The pet shown first was the _____.

The pet shown second was the _____.

The pet shown third was the _____.

The pet shown fourth was the _____.

The pet shown fifth was the _____.

The pet shown sixth was the _____.

Pet Pals

Skills:

Logic

Complete this logic puzzle to determine what kind of pet each person has. Use the clue on page 65, as well as the clues at the bottom of this page. Make an **X** in a box if a person does <u>not</u> own a certain pet. Write **Yes** in the box when you know which pet a person owns.

	Tom	Rascal	Smiley	Dipsey	Curly	Fido
Arlene						
Carlos						
Cecelia						
Chad						
Juan						
Nancy						

Clues

Curly and its owner do not have names that begin with the same letter.

Either Nancy or Cecilia own the fish.

The boy who owns the cat, Smiley's owner, and Chad live on the same street.

Arlene owns the turtle.

Juan owns either the rabbit or the snake.

Cecilia loves her pet's name: "Dipsey."

Math • EMC 4548 • ©2005 by Evan-Moor Corp.

Pet Pals

$$
\begin{array}{r} 2 \\ \times\ 3 \\ \hline \end{array}
\qquad
\begin{array}{r} 4 \\ \times\ 8 \\ \hline \end{array}
\qquad
\begin{array}{r} 9 \\ \times\ 3 \\ \hline \end{array}
\qquad
\begin{array}{r} 6 \\ \times\ 7 \\ \hline \end{array}
$$

$10 \div 2 =$ _____ $49 \div 7 =$ _____ $63 \div 9 =$ _____ $24 \div 6 =$ _____

What is the length of this line in inches? _____

What comes next in this pattern?

 _____

What comes next in this pattern?

89, 80, 71, 62, 53, _____

What place value does the digit 6 have in 47,986?

_____

List all the factors of 18.

_____

Plot the following ordered pairs on the coordinate graph.

A. (4, 9)

B. (13, 5)

C. (8, 2)

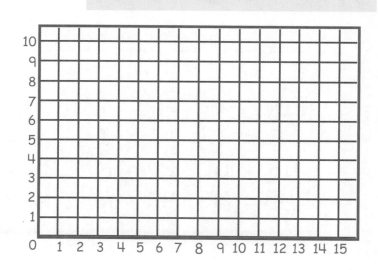

Skills:

Computation—
All Operations

Four children each have a different-colored library book, and each one checked out the book on a different day of the week. Solve the following problems to find when Kiki checked out her book. Use the key at the bottom of the page to see what letter corresponds to the answer, and then write it on the line below each problem.

$$\begin{array}{r} 5 \\ +\ 4 \\ \hline 9 \end{array} \qquad 21\div3 \qquad 45\div5 \qquad \begin{array}{r} 7 \\ \times\ 1 \\ \hline \end{array} \qquad\qquad \begin{array}{r} 5 \\ \times\ 3 \\ \hline \end{array} \qquad 45\div1 \qquad \begin{array}{r} 3 \\ \times\ 4 \\ \hline \end{array} \qquad \begin{array}{r} 5 \\ \times\ 3 \\ \hline \end{array} \qquad \begin{array}{r} 50 \\ -\ 41 \\ \hline \end{array} \qquad 24\div2 \qquad \begin{array}{r} 9 \\ \times\ 2 \\ \hline \end{array}$$

K ___ ___ ___   ___ ___ ___ ___ ___ ___ ___

$$\begin{array}{r} 50 \\ -\ 20 \\ \hline \end{array} \qquad \begin{array}{r} 9 \\ \times\ 3 \\ \hline \end{array} \qquad 12\div4 \qquad\qquad \begin{array}{r} 50 \\ -\ 5 \\ \hline \end{array} \qquad \begin{array}{r} 4 \\ \times\ 3 \\ \hline \end{array} \qquad \begin{array}{r} 8 \\ \times\ 8 \\ \hline \end{array} \qquad\qquad \begin{array}{r} 66 \\ -\ 10 \\ \hline \end{array} \qquad \begin{array}{r} 12 \\ +\ 18 \\ \hline \end{array} \qquad \begin{array}{r} 61 \\ -\ 31 \\ \hline \end{array} \qquad \begin{array}{r} 3 \\ \times\ 3 \\ \hline \end{array}$$

___ ___ ___   ___ ___ ___   ___ ___ ___ ___

$$\begin{array}{r} 23 \\ +\ 7 \\ \hline \end{array} \quad \begin{array}{r} 15 \\ +\ 5 \\ \hline \end{array} \quad \begin{array}{r} 50 \\ -\ 47 \\ \hline \end{array} \quad \begin{array}{r} 9 \\ \times\ 5 \\ \hline \end{array} \quad 12\div1 \quad \begin{array}{r} 32 \\ -\ 8 \\ \hline \end{array} \quad 36\div3 \quad \begin{array}{r} 6 \\ \times\ 2 \\ \hline \end{array} \quad \begin{array}{r} 66 \\ -\ 57 \\ \hline \end{array} \quad \begin{array}{r} 24 \\ -\ 12 \\ \hline \end{array} \quad \begin{array}{r} 39 \\ -\ 19 \\ \hline \end{array} \quad \begin{array}{r} 6 \\ +\ 12 \\ \hline \end{array}$$

___ ___ ___ ___ ___ ___ ___   ___ ___ ___ ___ ___

Key

3 = T	7 = I	9 = K	12 = E	15 = C
18 = D	20 = N	24 = W	27 = U	30 = O
45 = H	49 = M	56 = B	64 = R	

Math • EMC 4548 • ©2005 by Evan-Moor Corp.

At the Library

Use this line graph to answer the questions below.

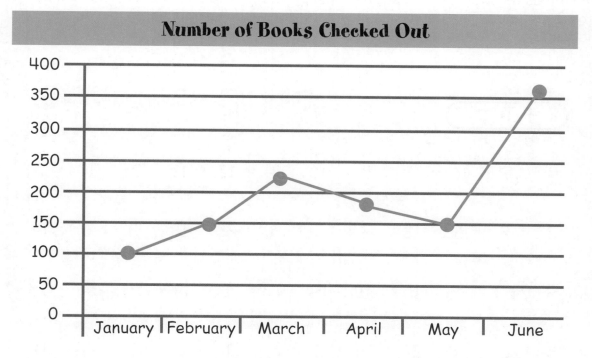

Number of Books Checked Out

Write how many children's books were checked out from the library during each month.

January	February	March	April	May	June
_____	_____	_____	_____	_____	_____

What is one reason there might have been more books checked out in March and in June?

_____

About how many books do you think might be checked out in July? Tell why.

_____

_____

_____

At the Library

Hidden Equations

Skills:

Equations—
Addition &
Subtraction

Hidden in the numbers below are at least 25 sets of numbers that can be written as an addition or a subtraction problem. The addition equations may have 2 or 3 addends. The equations may read forward (left to right), down, or diagonally. Circle the equations.

(2 + 5 = 7)	3	5	11	39	42	7	24	9	39
4	7	16	25	5	46	14	13	11	10	10	7
3	2	6	12	7	2	1	25	18	3	6	14
9	63	17	15	5	3	73	6	9	15	52	86
5	6	28	23	36	6	4	38	12	2	48	4
4	21	52	16	3	11	17	5	16	13	27	56
7	8	70	4	12	21	7	86	9	78	42	36
6	1	5	90	6	4	24	16	37	77	24	76
15	3	18	38	3	35	6	7	35	6	41	3
24	12	14	14	28	5	3	16	15	16	7	35
3	13	6	15	20	9	9	17	20	6	14	17
9	3	11	19	9	10	25	27	52	20	8	2

Skills:

Linear
Measurement

Use a centimeter ruler to measure the height and width of each of these covers to the nearest half-centimeter.

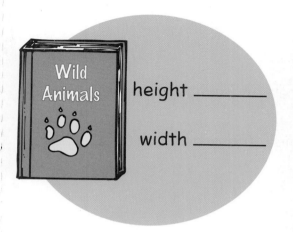

height _____

width _____

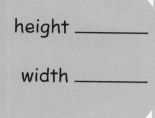

height _____

width _____

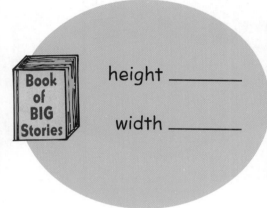

height _____

width _____

height _____

width _____

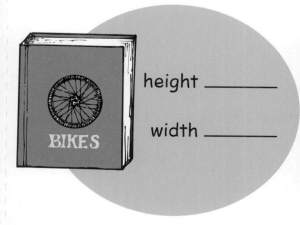

height _____

width _____

height _____

width _____

At the Library

How Many Blocks?

Each of the figures below is constructed using two different types of cubes. Some of the cubes are red and yellow while other cubes are green and blue. Given the pattern of alternating cubes in each layer, how many cubes of each type are used to construct each of these figures?

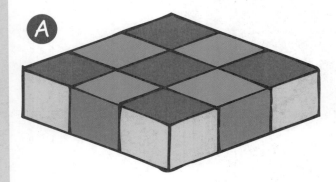

red and yellow cubes _____

blue and green cubes _____

red and yellow cubes _____

blue and green cubes _____

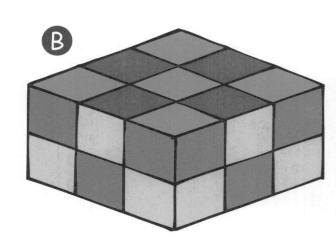

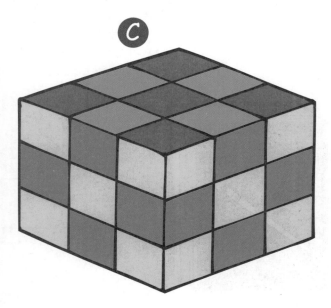

red and yellow cubes _____

blue and green cubes _____

Math • EMC 4548 • ©2005 by Evan-Moor Corp.

Jorge is looking for a book about scuba diving.
Solve each problem in order as you find the way through the maze.
Color the path through
the maze to help Jorge
find his book.

Skills:

Three-Digit
Number
Multiplied by
a Two-Digit
Number

At the Library

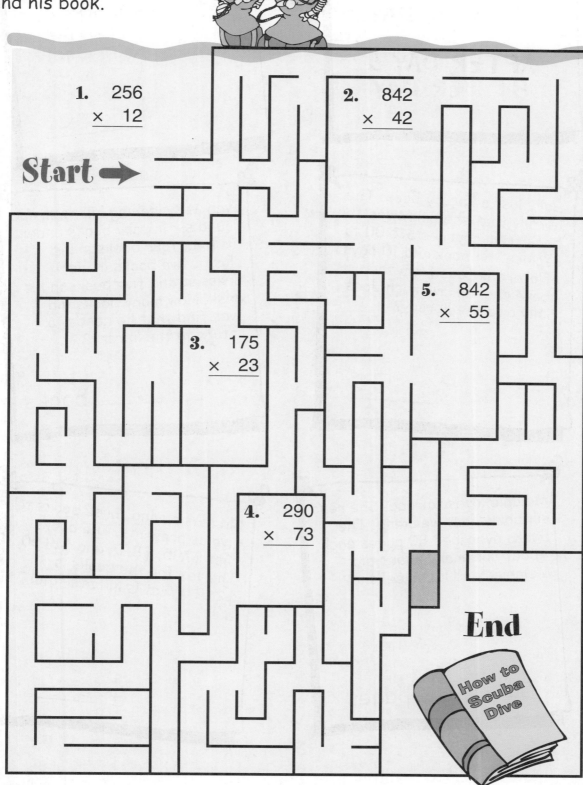

1. 256
   × 12

2. 842
   × 42

5. 842
   × 55

3. 175
   × 23

4. 290
   × 73

Start ➡

End

Skills:

Solving Word Problems

At the Library

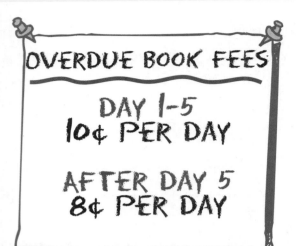

OVERDUE BOOK FEES

DAY 1-5
10¢ PER DAY

AFTER DAY 5
8¢ PER DAY

Mohammed just discovered that he has a book from the library that is 9 days overdue. Use the chart to the left to determine how much he owes the library in overdue fees.

$ _____

Sally lost a library book. The library that she borrowed the book from charges $15.00 to replace the book and 10 days of overdue fees from the above chart. How much does Sally owe the library?

$ _____

Ivan was cleaning his room and found six library books under his bed, four books in his closet, two books in his dresser, and five books in his desk. How many books did Ivan find that he needs to return to the library?

_____ books

Melanie loves to read. She read six books last weekend. The books averaged 80 pages each. About how many pages did Melanie read last weekend?

_____ pages

Nitza is buying three books to give as presents. The books cost $7.95, $8.97, and $19.50. The tax for the books is $2.19. What is Nitza's total bill?

$ _____

Round each of the following numbers to the place value listed.

For example, 298 rounded to the nearest hundred would be 300 because the digit to the right of the hundreds place is greater than or equal to five.

598 to the nearest hundred is _____ .

2,980 to the nearest thousand is _____ .

5,390 to the nearest thousand is _____ .

4,932 to the nearest hundred is _____ .

920 to the nearest hundred is _____ .

94,830 to the nearest thousand is _____ .

390 to the nearest hundred is _____ .

14,830 to the nearest ten thousand is _____ .

897 to the nearest ten is _____ .

98,700 to the nearest ten thousand is _____ .

985 to the nearest hundred is _____ .

158,970 to the nearest hundred thousand is _____ .

At the Library

The bookshelves below have books on them that are numbered in order. All of the books have been assigned different numbers. Some of the books are checked out. Write in the numbers of the books with missing numbers.

Note: The missing number must fall between the numbers of the books on either side of it. Sometimes the missing number is not a whole number. There may be more than one correct answer.

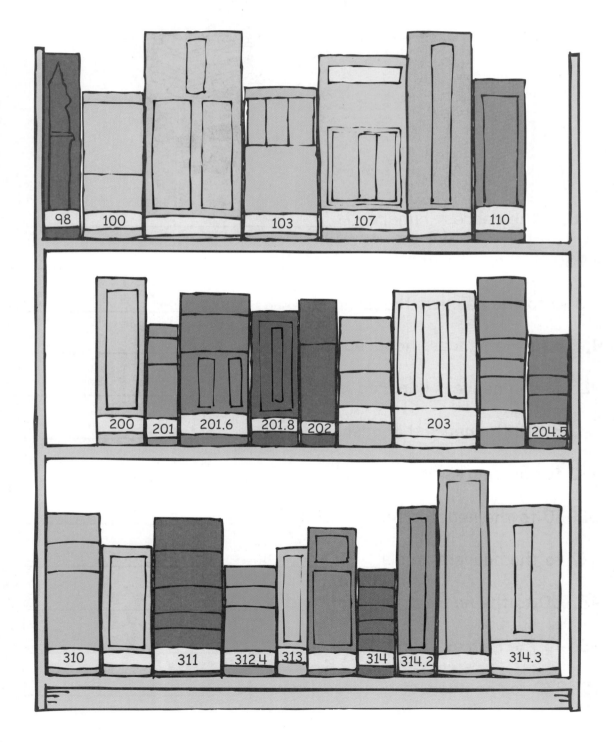

Math • EMC 4548 • ©2005 by Evan-Moor Corp.

Skills:

Multiples

Each of the clusters below represents the first few multiples of a given number. Complete the name of each cluster. What is the smallest multiple that is left out of the cluster?

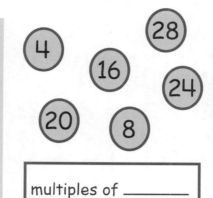

12 15 18 9 3

multiples of _____

left out _____

multiples of _____

left out _____

10 15 5 20 30

multiples of _____

left out _____

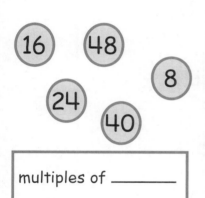
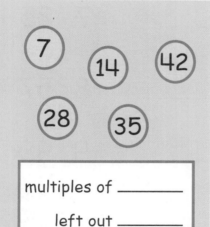
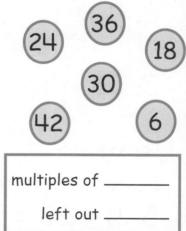

16 48 8 24 40

multiples of _____

left out _____

7 14 42 28 35

multiples of _____

left out _____

24 36 18 30 42 6

multiples of _____

left out _____

60 20 30 70 50 10

multiples of _____

left out _____

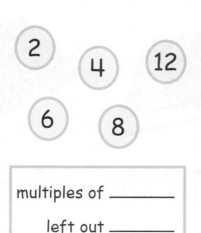

2 4 12 6 8

multiples of _____

left out _____

18 45 27 9 54

multiples of _____

left out _____

At the Library

Match It Up

Solve the problems below and match them up with the answers in the key. Write the answer letters in order of the problems to spell out the day the red book was checked out of the library.

Key

1 = T	3 = W	5 = N	9 = A	16 = E
24 = D	25 = O	26 = F	28 = M	37 = E
43 = D	50 = F	64 = S	72 = Y	

1. 12 ÷ 4 = _____

2. 4 x 4 = _____

3. 56 - 32 = _____

4. 14 - 9 = _____

5. 4 + 33 = _____

6. 8 x 8 = _____

7. 25 + 18 = _____

8. 57 - 48 = _____

9. 9 x 8 = _____

On what day was the red book checked out?

___ ___ ___ ___ ___ ___ ___ ___ ___

At the Library

TEST YOUR SKILLS

Read the graph. Fill in the correct circle to answer each question.

Books Checked Out of the School Library Last Week

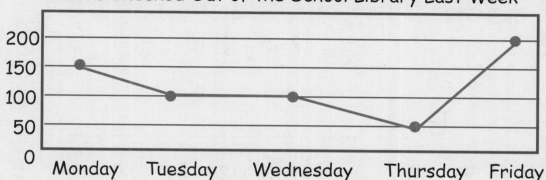

How many books were checked out on Tuesday?

  Ⓐ 200   Ⓒ 100
  Ⓑ 150   Ⓓ 50

On which day were the most books checked out?

  Ⓐ Tuesday   Ⓒ Monday
  Ⓑ Friday   Ⓓ Wednesday

How many books were checked out in all last week?

  Ⓐ 550   Ⓒ 600
  Ⓑ 400   Ⓓ 450

Multiply.

```
  256          842
x  12        x  42


  175          290
x  23        x  73
```

Round each of these numbers to the place value listed.

599 to the nearest hundred   _____

3,980 to the nearest thousand   _____

820 to the nearest hundred   _____

95,842 to the nearest ten thousand _____

148,251 to the nearest thousand   _____

Read the problem. Find the answer.

Melanie read 240 pages last weekend. Each book she read had an average of 80 pages. About how many books did Melanie read?

_____ books

What is the smallest multiple left out of this cluster?

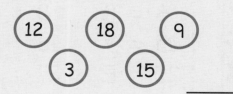

⑫   ⑱   ⑨

③   ⑮

_____

Break the Code

Skills:

Computation—
All Operations

On a trip to the city zoo, students discovered that there were differing numbers of animals in each of the cages. Solve the following problems to find a clue to help determine how many animals were in each of the cages. After solving all the problems, look at the key at the bottom of the page to see what letters correspond to the answers, and then write them on the lines below the problems.

$$
\begin{array}{cccccccc}
5 & 10 & 5 & & 1 & & 3 & 5 & 50 \\
+20 & \times 3 & \times 5 & 12 \div 2 & \times 3 & 10 \div 1 & \times 9 & \times 1 & -14 \\
\hline
25
\end{array}
$$

__E__ ___ ___ ___ ___ ___ ___ ___ ___

$$
\begin{array}{cccccccccc}
50 & 9 & & 66 & 12 & 61 & 9 & 50 & 5 & 9 \\
-40 & \times 3 & 8 \div 2 & -64 & +0 & -34 & +13 & -25 & \times 3 & \times 4 \\
\hline
\end{array}
$$

___ ___ ___   ___ ___ ___ ___ ___ ___ ___

$$
\begin{array}{cccccccc}
5 & & 50 & 3 & 12 & & 10 & 19 & & 6 \\
+7 & 16 \div 4 & -46 & \times 9 & +2 & 4 \div 2 & \times 2 & +6 & 72 \div 9 & \times 6 \\
\hline
\end{array}
$$

___ ___ ___   ___ ___ ___ ___ ___ ___ ___

$$
\begin{array}{cccccccc}
32 & 19 & 1 & 60 & 12 & 39 & 6 & & 66 & 12 \\
-16 & +8 & \times 5 & -57 & +13 & -21 & +4 & 9 \div 9 & -41 & +24 \\
\hline
\end{array}
$$

___ ___   ___ ___ ___   ___ ___ ___ ___ ___

Key

1 = G	2 = M	3 = H	4 = D	5 = T
6 = P	8 = R	10 = A	12 = O	14 = U
15 = Y	16 = I	18 = C	20 = B	22 = K
25 = E	27 = N	30 = L	36 = S	

8 × 6 | 48 | − 20

+ 2

÷ 5

Start at the zoo's main entrance. The first problem is 8 × 6. The first answer is written in the next box. Take that answer and subtract 20. Write that answer in the next empty box and continue this pattern around the path. After completing the problems, fill in the blanks below.

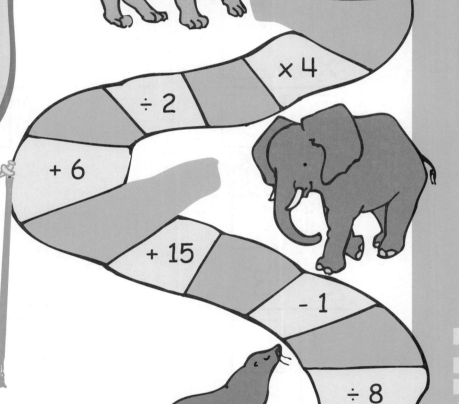

× 4

÷ 2

+ 6

+ 15

− 1

÷ 8

× 8

+ 24

− 9

Write in the answer that leads to these animals in the zoo:

Lions: _____

Elephants: _____

Seals: _____

Polar Bears: _____

The Zoo

Number Square Puzzler

Use the digits 0 through 9 to complete these number sentences. Use each number only once. Is there more than one possible solution? _____

0 1 2 3 4 5 6 7 8 9

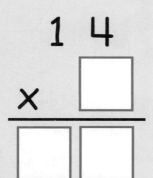

$$\begin{array}{r} 1\ 4 \\ \times\ \square \\ \hline \square\ \square \end{array}$$

$$\begin{array}{r} 2\ \square \\ \square \\ \times\ \square \\ \hline 1\ \square\ 5 \end{array}$$

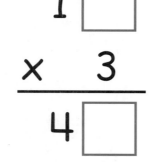

$$\begin{array}{r} 1\ \square \\ \times\ \ \ 3 \\ \hline 4\ \square \end{array}$$

$$\begin{array}{r} 1\ \square \\ \square \\ \times\ \square \\ \hline 1\ 5\ 3 \end{array}$$

The Zoo

A new home is being built for the monkeys.
Can you find the area of the new home?

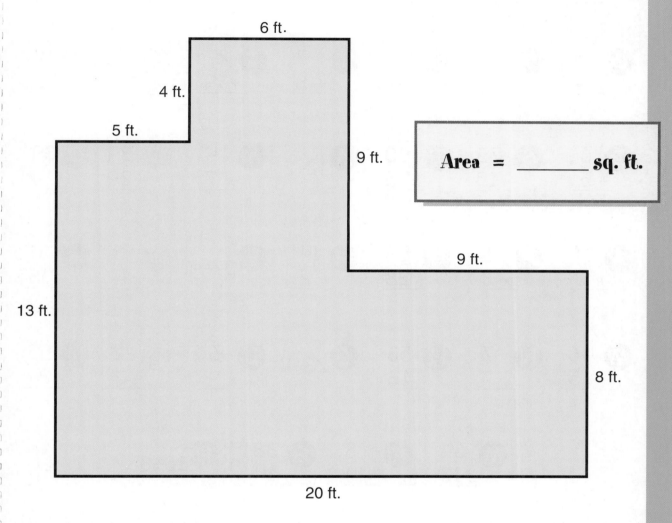

Area = _____ sq. ft.

Explain how you solved the problem.

_____

_____

_____

_____

_____

The Zoo

Put It in Order

Solve these problems:

U $\begin{array}{r} 13 \\ +12 \end{array}$ **E** $\begin{array}{r} 2 \\ \times 9 \end{array}$ **I** $\begin{array}{r} 20 \\ + 6 \end{array}$ **S** $\begin{array}{r} 46 \\ -12 \end{array}$ **S** $\begin{array}{r} 5 \\ +39 \end{array}$ **E** $\begin{array}{r} 3 \\ \times 7 \end{array}$ **C** $35 \div 7$

P $\begin{array}{r} 5 \\ \times 4 \end{array}$ **T** $\begin{array}{r} 6 \\ \times 6 \end{array}$ **E** $\begin{array}{r} 12 \\ - 4 \end{array}$ **T** $\begin{array}{r} 7 \\ + 8 \end{array}$ **T** $\begin{array}{r} 27 \\ +19 \end{array}$ **T** $8 \div 8$ **E** $\begin{array}{r} 49 \\ -10 \end{array}$

I $\begin{array}{r} 6 \\ + 5 \end{array}$ **S** $\begin{array}{r} 75 \\ -15 \end{array}$ **I** $\begin{array}{r} 10 \\ \times 5 \end{array}$ **A** $12 \div 2$ **N** $\begin{array}{r} 4 \\ \times 7 \end{array}$ **W** $\begin{array}{r} 39 \\ -29 \end{array}$ **O** $\begin{array}{r} 39 \\ + 4 \end{array}$

A $\begin{array}{r} 11 \\ \times 3 \end{array}$ **A** $\begin{array}{r} 6 \\ \times 8 \end{array}$ **H** $\begin{array}{r} 59 \\ -28 \end{array}$ **H** $\begin{array}{r} 14 \\ + 2 \end{array}$ **E** $27 \div 9$ **T** $\begin{array}{r} 3 \\ \times 4 \end{array}$ **H** $\begin{array}{r} 31 \\ -18 \end{array}$

M $\begin{array}{r} 46 \\ - 5 \end{array}$ **N** $\begin{array}{r} 7 \\ \times 7 \end{array}$ **H** $\begin{array}{r} 53 \\ -16 \end{array}$ **G** $28 \div 4$ **L** $\begin{array}{r} 6 \\ \times 9 \end{array}$ **S** $\begin{array}{r} 22 \\ + 7 \end{array}$ **N** $\begin{array}{r} 52 \\ -29 \end{array}$

M $\begin{array}{r} 64 \\ -13 \end{array}$ **A** $\begin{array}{r} 8 \\ +44 \end{array}$ **G** $\begin{array}{r} 38 \\ -14 \end{array}$ **H** $16 \div 8$

When all the problems have been completed, write the answers in order from smallest to largest. Then write the corresponding letter for each answer on the lines.

smallest

___ ___ ___   ___ ___ ___ ___   ___ ___ ___

___ ___ ___   ___ ___ ___ ___ ___ ___ ___

___ ___ ___   ___ ___ ___ ___ ___ ___ ___

___ ___ ___ ___ ___ ___ ___ ___   **largest**

The Zoo

Skills:

Calculating Area

The yellow figure below is an aerial view of a cage. Use the square grid to determine the number of tiles needed to cover the floor of the cage.

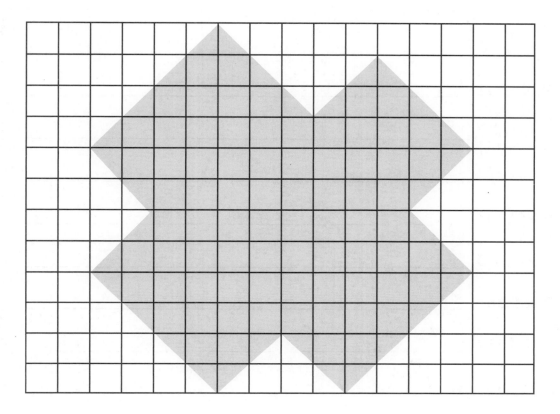

_____

square
floor tiles

Skills:

Place Value

Each number below contains the digit 3. On the line after each number, write the place value of the 3.

8,273 _____

31 _____

2,715,362 _____

30,000 _____

273 _____

420,398 _____

395,290 _____

3,905,862 _____

78,832 _____

36,459 _____

5,899,673 _____

438 _____

7,096,883 _____

7,376 _____

ones	thousands	millions
tens	ten thousands	
hundreds	hundred thousands	

The Zoo

Skills:

Multiples

Primes

Place Value

The number is:

▶ more than 12
▶ less than 20
▶ a multiple of 7

What is the number?

The number is:

▶ less than 100
▶ odd
▶ a multiple of 5
▶ more than 60

What **four** numbers could the number be?

The number is:

▶ more than 20
▶ even
▶ less than 23

What is the number?

The number is:

▶ a multiple of 8
▶ less than 100
▶ has a 5 in the tens place

What is the number?

The number is:

▶ more than 19
▶ less than 31
▶ a multiple of 9

What is the number?

The number is:

▶ prime
  (It can only be divided
  by 1 and itself.)
▶ greater than 20
▶ smaller than 28

What is the number?

The Zoo

Pathway of Sums

Begin at **Start**. Solve the problem and move through the yellow box with the correct sum to the next problem. Solve that problem and continue this pattern until you have reached **End** in the bottom-right corner. Trace your path as you go.

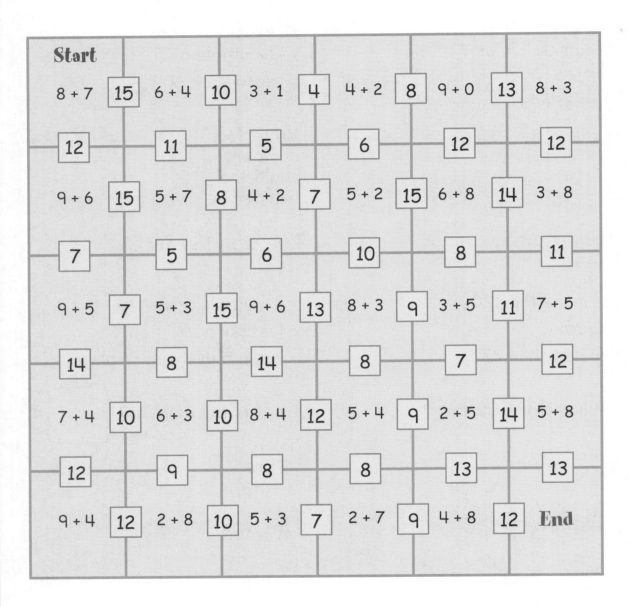

Start

8 + 7	15	6 + 4	10	3 + 1	4	4 + 2	8	9 + 0	13	8 + 3
12		11		5		6		12		12
9 + 6	15	5 + 7	8	4 + 2	7	5 + 2	15	6 + 8	14	3 + 8
7		5		6		10		8		11
9 + 5	7	5 + 3	15	9 + 6	13	8 + 3	9	3 + 5	11	7 + 5
14		8		14		8		7		12
7 + 4	10	6 + 3	10	8 + 4	12	5 + 4	9	2 + 5	14	5 + 8
12		9		8		8		13		13
9 + 4	12	2 + 8	10	5 + 3	7	2 + 7	9	4 + 8	12	**End**

What are all the factors for each of the following numbers?

Example: 20 — 1, 2, 4, 5, 10, 20

16 _____

12 _____

24 _____

What are all the common factors of 12, 16, and 24? (In other words, what same factors appear on all three lists?)

_____

What is the GCF (Greatest Common Factor) of 12, 16, and 24? (In other words, what is the largest common factor for all three numbers?)

_____

What are the first six multiples for each of the following numbers?

Example: 5 — 5, 10, 15, 20, 25, 30

3 _____

4 _____

6 _____

What is the LCM (Least Common Multiple) of 3, 4, and 6? (In other words, what is the smallest number that appears on all three lists?)

_____

Using a Grid

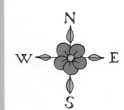

The grid below is a portion of a map. The Smiths' home is located at the ordered pair (17, 3). The Smiths start out at home and follow the directions written below to get to the zoo. (Each square represents one city block.) Find and mark the ordered pair of the zoo as well as the other landmarks listed below.

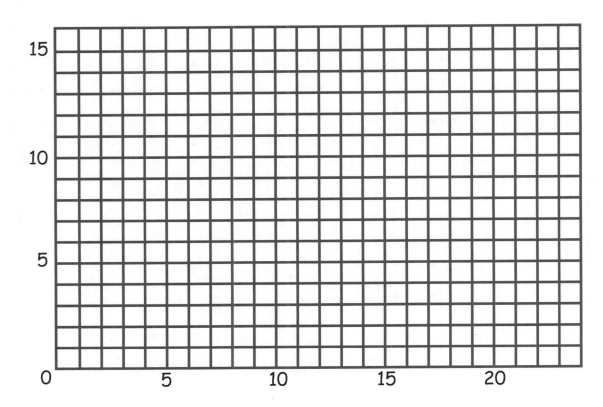

▶ Start at the Smiths' house (17, 3).

▶ Go 8 blocks north.

▶ Go east 3 blocks to the post office.

▶ Go south 9 blocks.

▶ Go west 11 blocks to the food market.

▶ Go north 8 blocks.

▶ Go west 5 blocks to the movie theater.

▶ Go north 5 blocks to the Gas'n Pump.

▶ Go east 19 blocks.

▶ Go south 1 block to the zoo.

What is the ordered pair for each of the following?

Post Office _____

Food Market _____

Movie Theater_____

Gas'n Pump _____

Zoo_____

The Zoo

Complete this logic puzzle to determine how many animals are in each cage. Use the clues on pages 90 and 94, as well as the clues at the bottom of this page.

	three	four	six	eight	nine	twelve
Elephants						
Monkeys						
Lions						
Zebras						
Seals						
Penguins						

Clues

There are more zebras than lions.

There are eight seals.

There are three more monkeys than zebras.

©2005 by Evan-Moor Corp. • EMC 4548 • Math

TEST YOUR SKILLS

$$\begin{array}{r} 5 \\ \times\ 9 \\ \hline \end{array} \qquad \begin{array}{r} 7 \\ \times\ 3 \\ \hline \end{array} \qquad \begin{array}{r} 4 \\ \times\ 3 \\ \hline \end{array} \qquad \begin{array}{r} 9 \\ \times\ 6 \\ \hline \end{array}$$

$20 \div 4 =$ _____ $14 \div 7 =$ _____ $20 \div 5 =$ _____ $18 \div 3 =$ _____

On the way to school, Sally walks past 14 houses. If the sidewalk in front of each house has an average of 20 cracks in it, how many cracks does Sally walk over on her way to school?

_____

What is 46,930 rounded to the nearest thousand?

_____

What are all the factors of 21 and 28?

_____

_____

What is the GCF of 21 and 28?

_____

What is the approximate area of the yellow figure?

_____

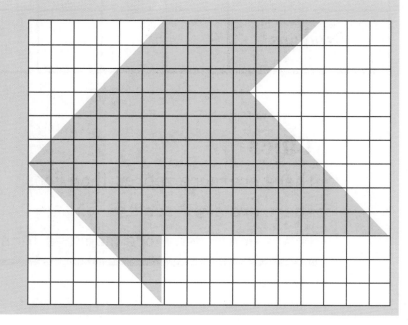

Math • EMC 4548 • ©2005 by Evan-Moor Corp.

Solve the following problems to find out if the tennis player is a boy or a girl. After solving all the problems, look at the key at the bottom of the page to see what letters correspond to the answers, and then write them on the lines below the problems.

$$\begin{array}{r} 5 \\ +22 \\ \hline 27 \end{array} \quad \begin{array}{r} 20 \\ \times 3 \\ \hline \end{array} \quad 25 \div 5 \qquad \begin{array}{r} 9 \\ \times 3 \\ \hline \end{array} \quad \begin{array}{r} 5 \\ \times 1 \\ \hline \end{array} \quad 32 \div 8 \quad \begin{array}{r} 1 \\ \times 4 \\ \hline \end{array} \quad \begin{array}{r} 7 \\ \times 4 \\ \hline \end{array} \quad \begin{array}{r} 50 \\ -41 \\ \hline \end{array}$$

$$\underline{T} \quad \underline{} \quad \underline{} \qquad \underline{} \quad \underline{} \quad \underline{} \quad \underline{} \quad \underline{} \quad \underline{}$$

$$\begin{array}{r} 50 \\ -43 \\ \hline \end{array} \quad \begin{array}{r} 4 \\ \times 3 \\ \hline \end{array} \quad \begin{array}{r} 10 \\ \times 5 \\ \hline \end{array} \quad \begin{array}{r} 66 \\ -21 \\ \hline \end{array} \quad \begin{array}{r} 2 \\ +3 \\ \hline \end{array} \quad \begin{array}{r} 61 \\ -31 \\ \hline \end{array} \qquad \begin{array}{r} 4 \\ \times 7 \\ \hline \end{array} \quad \begin{array}{r} 48 \\ -39 \\ \hline \end{array} \qquad \begin{array}{r} 5 \\ \times 10 \\ \hline \end{array}$$

$$\underline{} \quad \underline{} \quad \underline{} \quad \underline{} \quad \underline{} \quad \underline{} \qquad \underline{} \quad \underline{} \qquad \underline{}$$

$$9 \div 9 \quad \begin{array}{r} 15 \\ +35 \\ \hline \end{array} \quad \begin{array}{r} 50 \\ -38 \\ \hline \end{array} \quad \begin{array}{r} 1 \\ \times 5 \\ \hline \end{array}$$

$$\underline{} \quad \underline{} \quad \underline{} \quad \underline{}$$

Key

1 = M	4 = N	5 = E	7 = P
9 = S	12 = L	27 = T	28 = I
30 = R	45 = Y	50 = A	60 = H

Reading a Thermometer

Read each thermometer. Notice that the scale on the red and yellow thermometers is different. You will also notice that some of the readings are between numbers on the scale. What is the best estimate for each temperature reading?

A _____

B _____

C _____

D _____

E _____

F _____

G _____

H _____

I _____

J _____

K _____

Summer Sports

Math • EMC 4548 • ©2005 by Evan-Moor Corp.

For each problem below, give an **estimate** for each answer. Do <u>not</u> compute the exact answer.

What is a good estimate for 11 x 31? Explain how you got your estimate.	What is a good estimate for the sum of 299 and 503? Explain why your sum is a good estimate.
_____ estimate	_____ estimate
What is a good estimate for 604 - 98? Explain how you got your estimate.	What is a good estimate for the product of 8,013 and 2? Explain how you got your estimate.
_____ estimate	_____ estimate
What is a good estimate for how many times 9 goes into 3,000? Explain why your answer is a good estimate.	What is a good estimate for 951 + 240? Explain how you got your estimate.
_____ estimate	_____ estimate

Summer Sports

Hidden Equations

Skills:

Equations—
Multiplication
& Division

Hidden in the numbers below are at least 25 sets of numbers that can be written as a multiplication or division problem. The equations may read forward (left to right), down, or diagonally. Circle the equations.

(48 ÷ 8 = 6)	7	25	5	5	3	2	27	43	6
24	3	3	4	12	13	10	5	61	9	7	8
15	29	4	7	3	2	1	6	3	4	18	11
3	16	8	2	3	9	5	30	9	3	2	31
5	3	5	4	1	21	3	8	42	2	7	14
5	9	45	53	5	4	12	3	7	24	90	13
31	3	4	28	7	3	82	20	6	10	6	7
27	7	7	41	35	10	2	8	7	3	6	4
3	4	2	47	18	5	4	4	16	8	30	17
9	41	6	40	3	2	5	1	8	20	56	6
7	6	12	5	7	15	6	4	4	5	7	3
3	6	18	8	61	73	2	17	23	4	1	2

Summer Sports

Skills:

Coordinate
Graphing

Plot the ordered pairs of numbers on the graph in the order in which they are listed, connecting them with straight lines. Start each new set of points with a new line.

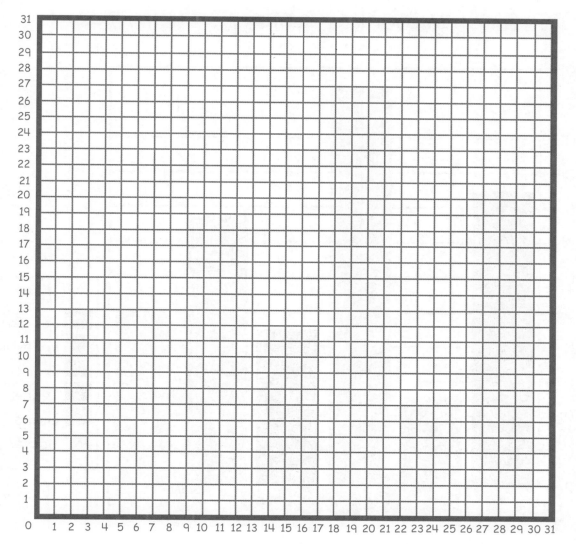

▶ (5, 5) (4, 7) (10, 7) (13, 13) (21, 13)
(18, 22) (17, 22) (17, 23) (19, 23) (23, 13)
(24, 13) (26, 11) (28, 7) (28, 5) line ends

▶ (5, 9) (6, 14) (6, 18) (8, 25) (9, 25) (10, 26)
(9, 27) (9, 28) (10, 30) (13, 30) (14, 28)
(14, 27) (13, 26) (12, 26) (11, 25) (12, 24)
(18, 24) (19, 23) (11, 23) (9, 16) (7, 9) (7, 8)
(9, 8) (9, 7) line ends

▶ (0, 5) (31, 5) line ends

▶ (11, 9) (7, 9) line ends

▶ (9, 16) (9, 9) line ends

▶ (5, 7) (5, 9) (4, 9) (4, 7) line ends

Summer Sports

Counting Spectators

The graph below represents the number of spectators that were at each event on a certain Saturday. Use the graph to answer the following questions.

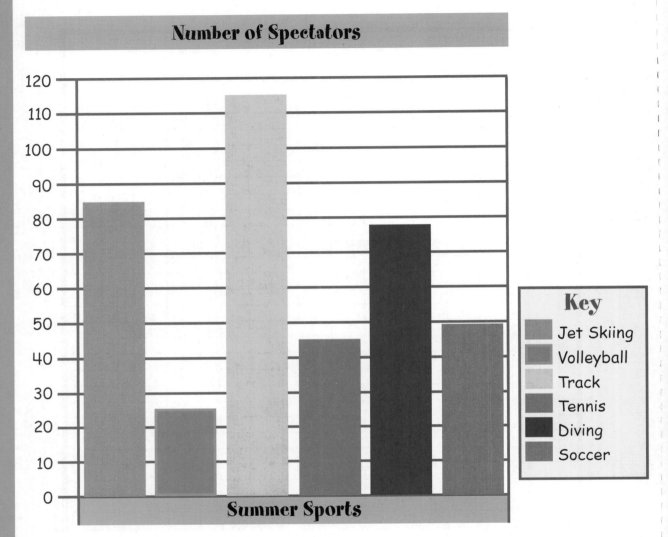

Which sport had the fewest spectators? About how many spectators were at this sporting event? _____ _____

Which sport had the most spectators? About how many spectators were at this sporting event? _____ _____

About how many more spectators were at the jet skiing event than the diving event? _____

About how many spectators were at all six events? _____

Shown below is the new billboard at the entrance to the ballpark. Below the billboard are the names of some two-dimensional and three-dimensional shapes. Locate each of the shapes in the picture. Color the two-dimensional shapes blue and the three-dimensional shapes red.

| cylinder | star | triangular pyramid |
| cube | pentagon | circle |

Summer Sports

First Prize

Plot the ordered pairs of numbers on the graph in the order in which they are listed, connecting them with straight lines. Start each new set of points with a new line.

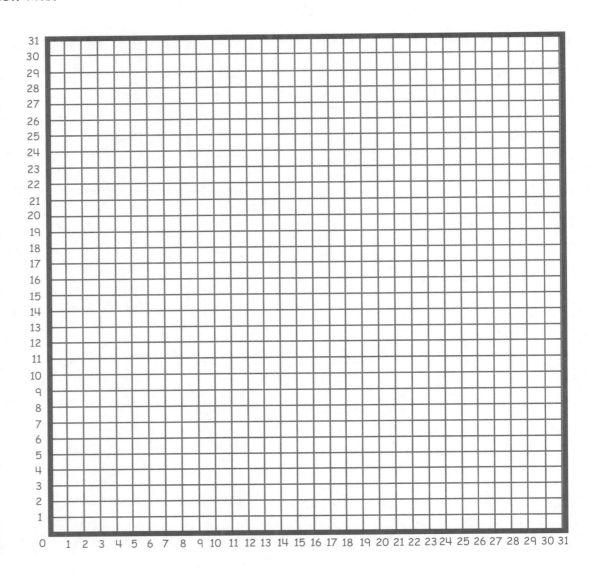

▶ (16, 6) (7, 21) (5, 21) (2, 24) (2, 27) (4, 29) (7, 29) (10, 26) (10, 24) (21, 11) (16, 12) (16, 6) line ends

▷ (22, 17) (22, 22) (18, 23) (22, 24) (22, 28) (24, 25) (28, 26) (26, 23) (28, 19) (25, 21) (22, 17) line ends

▶ (6, 23) (8, 25) line ends

▶ (4, 25) (4, 27) (7, 24) line ends

UNIT 9   Math • EMC 4548 • ©2005 by Evan-Moor Corp.

John needs to get from the park entrance to the stadium. In order to walk along any of the paths, he has to give the gatekeeper the number of tickets noted on each path. He has 73 tickets and must use all of them in order to enter the stadium. What paths must he take to the stadium? Is there more than one possible path? _____

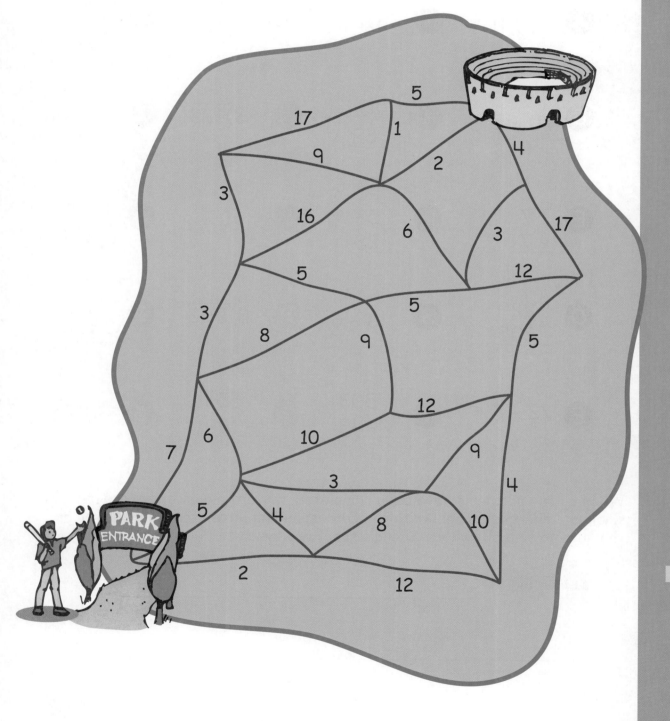

Summer Sports

Put It in Order

Skills:

Computation—
All Operations

Solve these problems.

P 80 ÷ 4   **S** 5)175   **E** 171 − 99   **H** 49 ÷ 7

A 7)91   **T** 8)216   **H** 112 − 68   **T** 39 + 3

S 70 ÷ 5   **A** 141 − 89   **N** 3)123   **I** 10)100

E 7 × 7   **R** 53 − 28   **L** 24 ÷ 2   **W** 169 − 118

O 229 − 205   **S** 18 ÷ 6   **R** 8)592   **I** 360 − 329

E 72 ÷ 8   **T** 503 − 443   **I** 553 − 514   **S** 6)108

When all the problems have been completed, write the answers in order from smallest to largest. Then write the corresponding letter for each answer on the lines to find out where Sheila's sport is played.

smallest ___ ___ ___ ___ ___ ___ ___

___ ___ ___ ___ ___ ___ ___ ___

___ ___ ___ ___ ___ **largest**

Summer Sports

Find the Color and Number

Use the following clues to determine what whole number goes in each region and what color it should be. All the numbers are less than 10. Color the figure and write in the numbers.

Skills:

Properties

Number Relationships

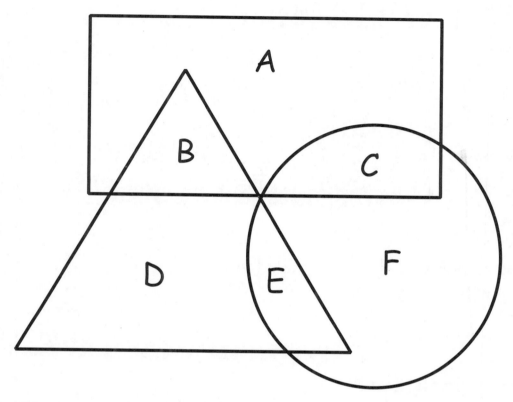

▶ The sum of the triangle is 16.

▶ The region that is in the circle and the rectangle is colored green.

▶ The rectangle has orange, yellow, and green regions.

▶ The orange region is the number 5.

▶ The product of the B section and the blue section is 10.

▶ The 9 region is black.

▶ A is yellow.

▶ The sum of the rectangle is 17.

▶ E is black.

▶ The sum of the circle is 24.

▶ The sum of A and B is 9.

▶ F is red.

TEST YOUR SKILLS

Fill in the circle of the correct answer.

171
- 94

Ⓐ 76
Ⓑ 87
Ⓒ 77
Ⓓ 85

553
- 274

Ⓐ 275
Ⓑ 279
Ⓒ 278
Ⓓ 269

503
- 443

Ⓐ 80
Ⓑ 60
Ⓒ 70
Ⓓ 50

365
- 258

Ⓐ 106
Ⓑ 105
Ⓒ 107
Ⓓ 108

3)39

Ⓐ 23
Ⓑ 11
Ⓒ 12
Ⓓ 13

5)250

Ⓐ 40
Ⓑ 50
Ⓒ 60
Ⓓ 30

6)432

Ⓐ 76
Ⓑ 74
Ⓒ 72
Ⓓ 75

4)256

Ⓐ 64
Ⓑ 44
Ⓒ 56
Ⓓ 48

Plot the ordered pairs.
Connect them with straight lines.

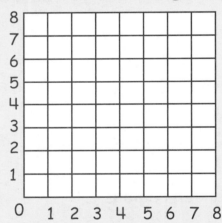

(2, 1) (2, 6) (3, 6) (3, 4) (5, 4) (5, 6)
(6, 6) (6, 1) (5, 1) (5, 3) (3, 3) (3, 1) (2, 1)

What letter did you make? _____

Match.

   •

   •

   •

   •

   •

• triangular pyramid

• pentagon

• cylinder

• circle

• cube

Write two division facts for each model.

____ ÷ ____ = ____

____ ÷ ____ = ____

____ ÷ ____ = ____

____ ÷ ____ = ____

Skills:

Computation—
All Operations

David   Julie   Kevin   Kristin   Wendy

Five people each own a different video arcade. Solve the following problems to find the first clue to help determine who owns each of the video stores. After solving all the problems, look at the key at the bottom of the page to see what letters correspond to the answers, and then write them on the lines below the problems.

$$\begin{array}{c}5\\+\ 1\\\hline 6\end{array}\qquad\begin{array}{c}9\\\times\ 9\\\hline\end{array}\qquad 10\div5\qquad\begin{array}{c}9\\\times\ 8\\\hline\end{array}\qquad\begin{array}{c}10\\\times\ 10\\\hline\end{array}\qquad\begin{array}{c}4\\\times\ 5\\\hline\end{array}\qquad 36\div6\qquad 8\div4\qquad\begin{array}{c}37\\-\ 22\\\hline\end{array}$$

W __ · __ __ __   __ __ __ __

$$\begin{array}{c}50\\-\ 5\\\hline\end{array}\qquad\begin{array}{c}8\\\times\ 7\\\hline\end{array}\qquad\begin{array}{c}8\\\times\ 9\\\hline\end{array}\qquad\begin{array}{c}102\\-\ 21\\\hline\end{array}\qquad\begin{array}{c}17\\+\ 3\\\hline\end{array}\qquad\begin{array}{c}61\\-\ 31\\\hline\end{array}\qquad\begin{array}{c}7\\\times\ 8\\\hline\end{array}\qquad\begin{array}{c}29\\+41\\\hline\end{array}\qquad\begin{array}{c}93\\+\ 7\\\hline\end{array}$$

__ __ __ __ __   __ __ __ __

Key

2 = N	6 = W	7 = A	15 = S
20 = O	30 = C	45 = V	56 = I
70 = T	72 = D	81 = E	100 = Y

Guess the Mystery Number

Skills:

Properties

Number
Relationships

The number:

- ▶ is even
- ▶ is more than 100
- ▶ is less than 200
- ▶ has a 7 in the tens place
- ▶ is divisible by 5

What is the number?

The number:

- ▶ has the digit 2 somewhere in it
- ▶ is even
- ▶ is less than 300
- ▶ is a multiple of 10
- ▶ has a 0 in the tens place

What is the number?

The number:

- ▶ has a 4 in the ones place
- ▶ has the digit 5 somewhere in it
- ▶ is greater than 800
- ▶ is less than 900

What is the number?

The number:

- ▶ is less than 100
- ▶ is more than 60
- ▶ is odd
- ▶ is the product of one number times itself
- ▶ has the digit 8 somewhere in it

What is the number?

The number:

- ▶ is more than 300
- ▶ is 40 less than 500
- ▶ is a multiple of 10
- ▶ is even

What is the number?

Video Arcades

For each of the function machines below, **two** rules could be followed to obtain the OUTPUT. For example, on letter A, the INPUT is 8 and the OUTPUT is 24. One rule could be to take the INPUT and multiply by 3 to get the OUTPUT. Another rule could be to add 16 to the INPUT to get the OUTPUT. These rules have been written on the function machine for letter A. Write two rules on each of the other function machines.

8 input
×3
+16
output 24

6 input
output 24

4 input
output 32

2 input
output 6

7 input
output 14

3 input
output 24

The following function machines have only **one** rule. Notice that three different numbers have been fed into the function machine and three different numbers have come out the other side. The colors correspond, so the green INPUT number corresponds to the green OUTPUT number. Write one rule on each function machine.

3 7 5 input
output 25 23 27

4 2 9 input
output 12 27 6

Video Arcades

Add Them Up

Find the sum for each of the following,

1. 208 + 520 + 286 + 826 = ____

2. 601 + 843 + 826 + 825 = ____

3. 926 + 482 + 82 = ____

4. 865 + 22 + 862 + 93 = ____

5.
```
  826
  835
  731
+ 651
```

6.
```
  561
  526
  349
+ 496
```

7.
```
  592
  103
  501
+ 600
```

8.
```
  506
   59
  496
+  34
```

9.
```
  496
  182
  496
+ 768
```

10.
```
  792
  852
  816
  195
+ 463
```

Video Arcades

Math · EMC 4548 · ©2005 by Evan-Moor Corp.

Skills:

Equations

Use the digits 0 through 9 to complete these number sentences. Use each number only once. Is there more than one possible solution? _____

0 1 2 3 4 5 6 7 8 9

$$
\begin{array}{r}
1\ \square \\
\times\quad 6 \\
\hline
\square\ 0
\end{array}
$$

$$
\begin{array}{r}
\square\ 5 \\
\times\quad 3 \\
\hline
\square\ \square
\end{array}
$$

$$
36 \div \square = \square
$$

$$
\begin{array}{r}
\square\ 6\ 3 \\
\times\quad \square \\
\hline
4\ \square\ 9
\end{array}
$$

Video Arcades

Reading a Bar Graph

The graph below represents the number of boys and girls who went to each of the video arcades last Saturday. Use the graph to answer the questions.

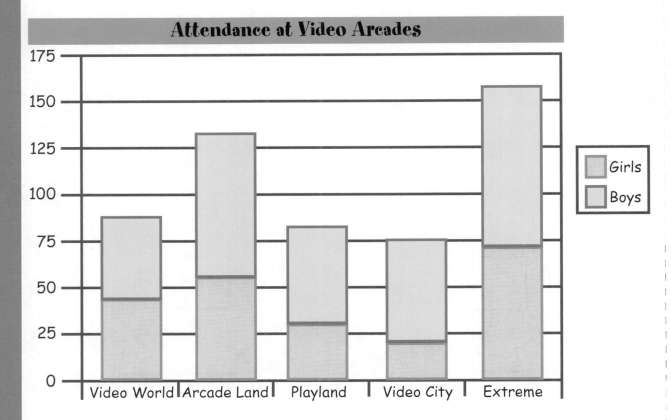

Which arcade did the highest number of girls attend? _____

About how many girls attended this arcade? _____

Which arcade did the highest number of boys attend? _____

About how many boys attended this arcade? _____

Which arcade did the fewest number of girls attend? _____

About how many girls attended this arcade? _____

Which arcade did the fewest number of boys attend? _____

About how many boys attended this arcade? _____

Video Arcades

Put It in Order

Computation—
All Operations

Solve these problems.

W 5
× 4

E 34
− 9

Y 27
+ 4

L 49÷7

N 6
+ 15

B 10
× 3

D 9
× 3

A 32
+ 3

D 12
+ 0

A 44
+ 6

F 3
+ 39

Y 24÷4

S 5
× 3

L 88
− 28

A 36÷4

I 31
− 18

M 51
− 5

A 32÷8

N 5
× 2

E 101
− 29

P 8÷8

O 6
× 3

E 59
− 14

L 24÷8

When all the problems have been completed, write the answers in order from least to the greatest. Then write the corresponding letter for each answer on the lines.

least ___ ___ ___ ___ ___ ___ ___ ___

___ ___ ___ ___ ___ ___ ___ ___

___ ___ ___ ___ ___ ___ **greatest**

Video Arcades

©2005 by Evan-Moor Corp. • EMC 4548 • Math

UNIT 10

121

Numbers and Words

Draw a straight line to connect each numerical form with its corresponding word form.

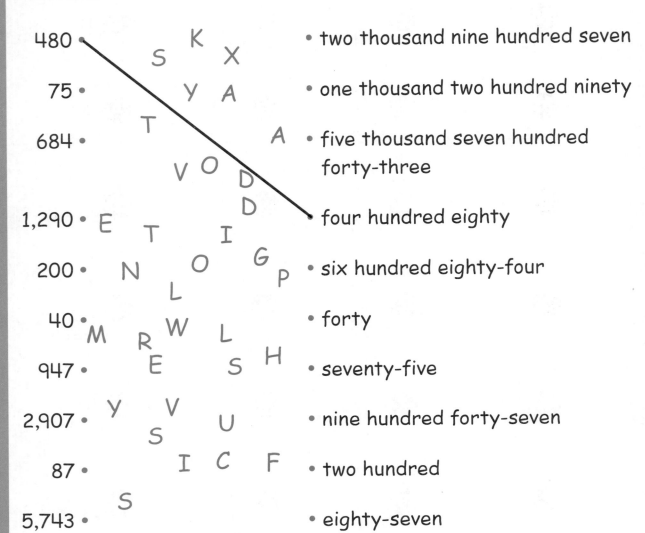

480 •

75 •

684 •

1,290 •

200 •

40 •

947 •

2,907 •

87 •

5,743 •

• two thousand nine hundred seven

• one thousand two hundred ninety

• five thousand seven hundred forty-three

• four hundred eighty

• six hundred eighty-four

• forty

• seventy-five

• nine hundred forty-seven

• two hundred

• eighty-seven

Write the letters that are inside each closed figure. These letters can be arranged into the name of the video arcade that is owned by Kevin. Which arcade does Kevin own?

HINT:
A closed figure is a polygon with straight lines on all sides without any "invisible" sides to the shape.

Video Arcades

Skills:

Area

Perimeter

Below is a map of Video World, the arcade that has the best games in town. The owner of Video World wants to do some remodeling. What is the area of that part of Video World currently covered with gray carpet? How much wallpaper border will it take to go around the gray-carpeted room? In other words, what is the perimeter of the gray-carpeted room?

Area _____   Perimeter _____

60 feet

36 feet

24 feet

24 feet

Office

108 feet

24 feet

48 feet

60 feet

Video Arcades

Star Trapper

In the game Star Trapper, points are awarded for every star on the screen. The key shows the point value for each type of star. An airplane on the screen counts against a player's score. Below are three screens from Star Trapper. Which game has the highest score? _____

Point value for each item

✦ = 8   ☆ = 10   ✺ = 6

✳ = 15   ✶ = 5   ❋ = 3

✈ = ⁻20   ✷ = 2   ✈ = ⁻50

Game 1

Game 2

Game 3

Video Arcades

124

UNIT 10

Math • EMC 4548 • ©2005 by Evan-Moor Corp.

Understanding Fractions and Decimals

For each of the following, write the fraction and decimal that represents the shaded region. The first one has been done for you.

$\dfrac{8}{10}$ 0.8

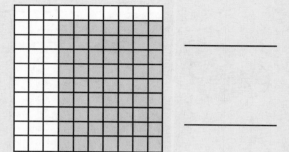

_____

_____

_____   _____

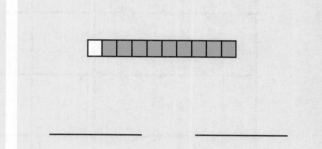   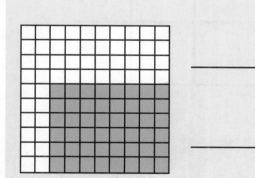

_____   _____

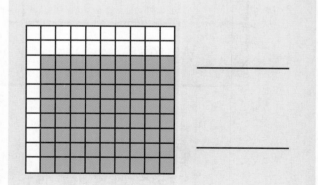   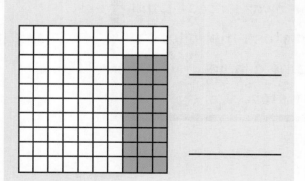

_____   _____

_____

_____   _____

Video Arcades

Skills:

Logic

Complete this logic puzzle to determine who owns each of the video game stores. Use the clues on pages 115, 121, and 122, as well as the clues at the bottom of this page.

ZING! BEEP BANG!

	Video World	Arcade Land	Playland	Video City	Extreme
David					
Julie					
Kevin					
Kristin					
Wendy					

Clues

David does not own Extreme.

Neither Julie nor Kevin owns Arcade Land.

Kristin has owned her store the longest.

Arcade Land is owned by a male.

Playland is the newest store.

Video Arcades

Note: Use this page and page 128 after your child has completed through page 126.

TEST YOUR SKILLS

$$\begin{array}{r} 7 \\ \times\,2 \\ \hline \end{array} \qquad \begin{array}{r} 8 \\ \times\,9 \\ \hline \end{array} \qquad \begin{array}{r} 5 \\ \times\,5 \\ \hline \end{array} \qquad \begin{array}{r} 2 \\ \times\,4 \\ \hline \end{array}$$

$40 \div 8 =$ _____ $56 \div 8 =$ _____ $35 \div 5 =$ _____ $24 \div 4 =$ _____

What value is represented by the X on this number line? _____

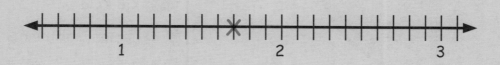

What is a good estimate of 11 x 42? _____
Explain how you got your estimate.

_____

_____

Write two rules for each function machine.

In this graph, which soda was liked the most? _____

About what percentage of students liked that soda? _____

Favorite Sodas

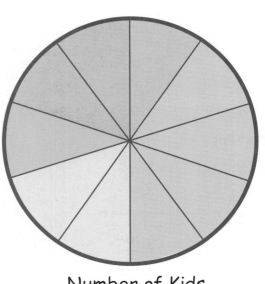

Number of Kids

Key
- Fizzy Soda
- Strawberry Sizzle
- Bubbly Banana
- Kid Kola
- Lemon Lightning

Write the number 3,691 in word form. _____

Write the fraction and decimal that represent this shaded region.

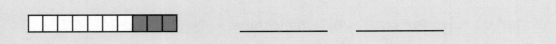

_____   _____

Give the area and the perimeter of the shape below.

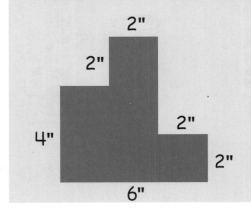

area _____

perimeter _____

Tracking Form

Topic	Color in each page you complete.						
A Day of Fun	3	4	5	6	7	8	9
	10	11	12	13	14		
Family Reunion	15	16	17	18	19	20	21
	22	23	24	25	26	27	
Music, Music, Music	28	29	30	31	32	33	34
	35	36	37	38	39		
The Candy Sale	40	41	42	43	44	45	46
	47	48	49	50	51	52	
Winter Break	53	54	55	56	57	58	59
	60	61	62	63	64		
Pet Pals	65	66	67	68	69	70	71
	72	73	74	75	76	77	
At the Library	78	79	80	81	82	83	84
	85	86	87	88	89		
The Zoo	90	91	92	93	94	95	96
	97	98	99	100	101	102	
Summer Sports	103	104	105	106	107	108	109
	110	111	112	113	114		
Video Arcades	115	116	117	118	119	120	121
	122	123	124	125	126	127	128

Red numbers indicate Test Your Skills pages.

Answer Key

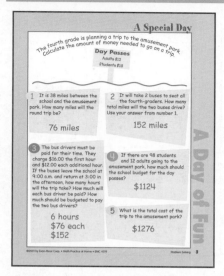

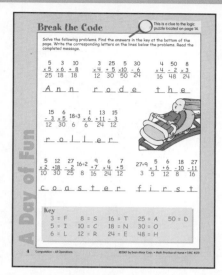

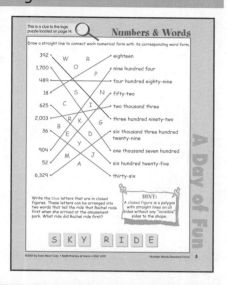

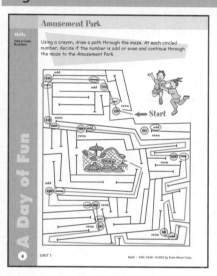

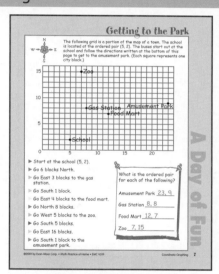

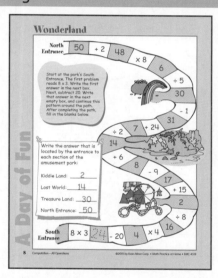

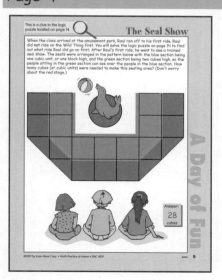

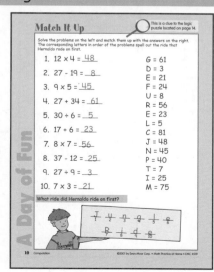

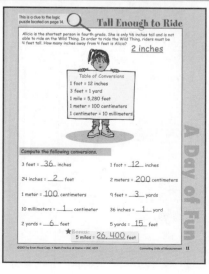

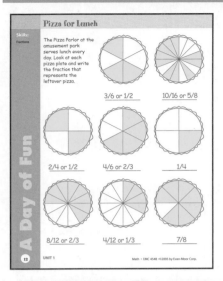

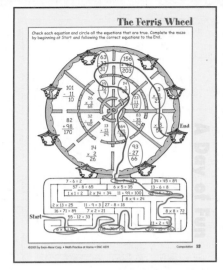

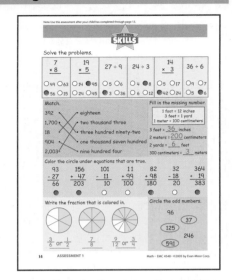

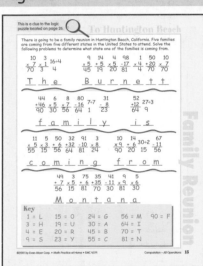

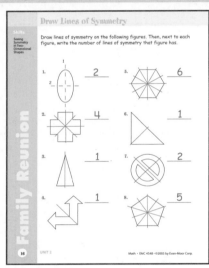

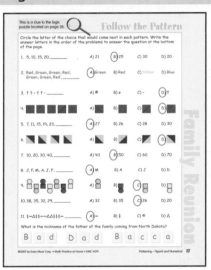

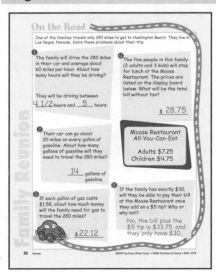

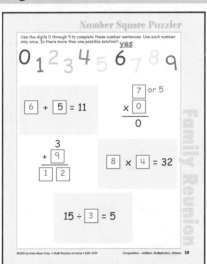

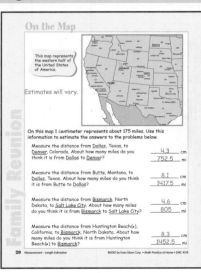

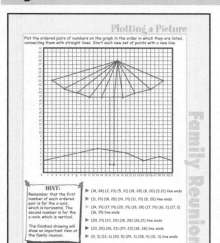

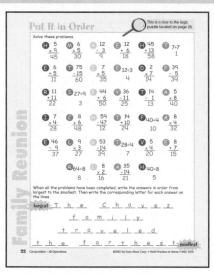

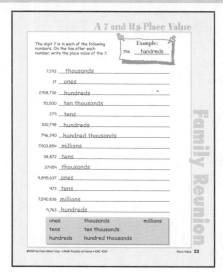

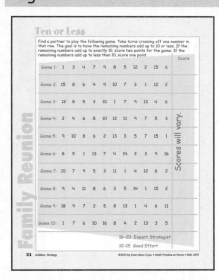

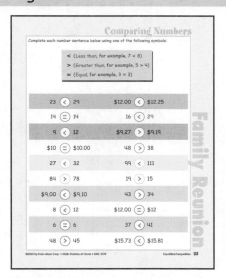

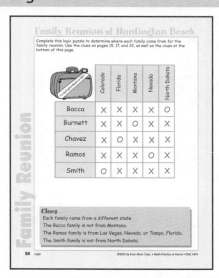

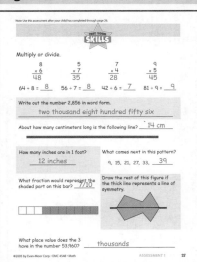

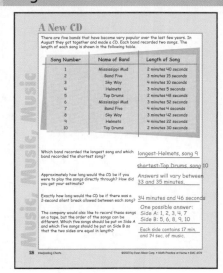

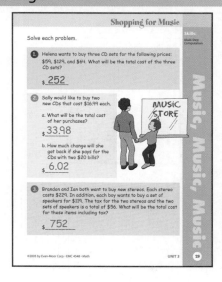

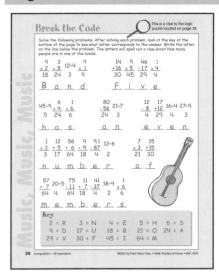

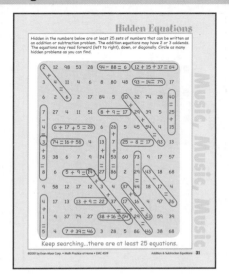

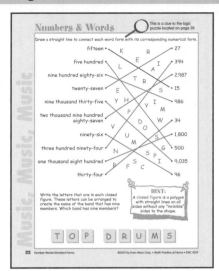

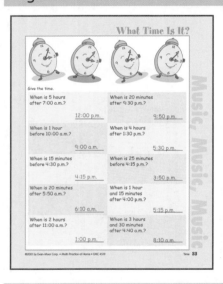

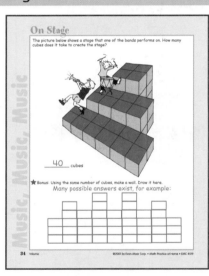

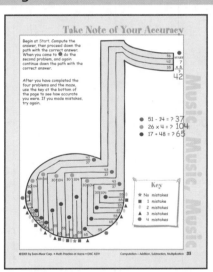

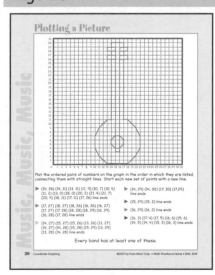

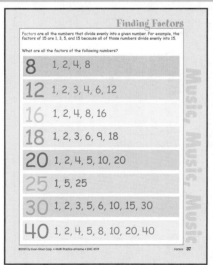

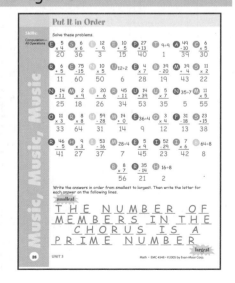

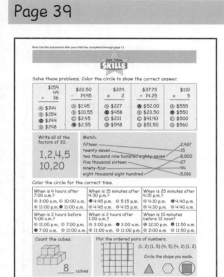

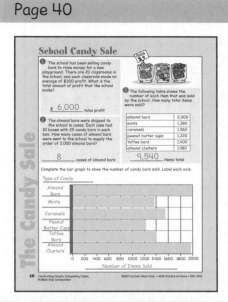

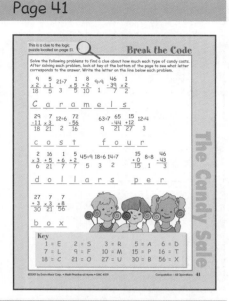

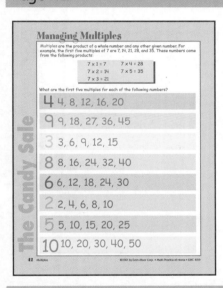

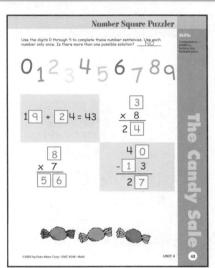

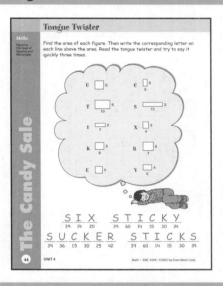

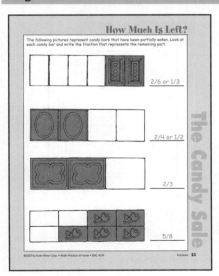

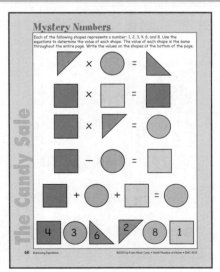

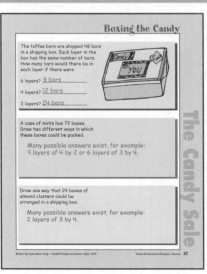

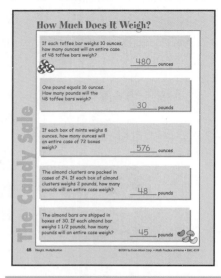

Page 48 — How Much Does It Weigh?

If each toffee bar weighs 10 ounces, how many ounces will an entire case of 48 toffee bars weigh? **480** ounces

One pound equals 16 ounces. How many pounds will the 48 toffee bars weigh? **30** pounds

If each box of mints weighs 8 ounces, how many ounces will an entire case of 72 boxes weigh? **576** ounces

The almond clusters are packed in cases of 24. If each box of almond clusters weighs 2 pounds, how many pounds will an entire case weigh? **48** pounds

The almond bars are shipped in boxes of 30. If each almond bar weighs 1 1/2 pounds, how many pounds will an entire case weigh? **45** pounds

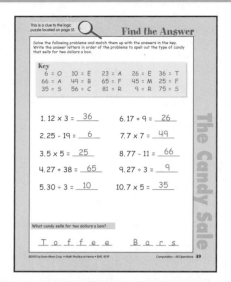

Page 49 — Find the Answer

This is a clue to the logic puzzle located on page 51.
Solve the following problems and match them up with the answers in the key. Write the answer letters in order of the problems to spell out the type of candy that sells for two dollars a box.

Key

6 = O	10 = E	23 = A	26 = E	36 = T
66 = A	49 = B	65 = F	45 = M	25 = F
35 = S	56 = C	81 = R	9 = R	75 = S

1. 12 × 3 = **36**　　6. 17 + 9 = **26**

2. 25 - 19 = **6**　　7. 7 × 7 = **49**

3. 5 × 5 = **25**　　8. 77 - 11 = **66**

4. 27 + 38 = **65**　　9. 27 ÷ 3 = **9**

5. 30 ÷ 3 = **10**　　10. 7 × 5 = **35**

What candy sells for two dollars a box?

T o f f e e   B a r s

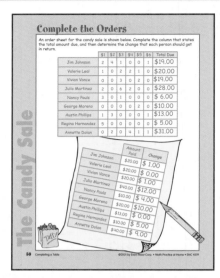

Page 50 — Complete the Orders

An order sheet for the candy sale is shown below. Complete the column that states the total amount due, and then determine the change that each person should get in return.

	$1	$2	$3	$4	$5	$6	Total Due
Jim Johnson	2	4	1	0	0	1	$19.00
Valerie Leal	1	0	2	2	1	0	$20.00
Vivian Vance	0	0	3	0	2	0	$19.00
Julio Martinez	2	0	6	2	0	0	$28.00
Nancy Pauls	0	0	1	0	0	0	$ 6.00
George Moreno	0	0	0	0	2	0	$10.00
Austin Phillips	1	3	0	0	0	1	$13.00
Regina Hernandez	5	0	0	0	0	0	$ 5.00
Annette Dolan	0	2	0	4	1	1	$31.00

	Amount Paid	Change
Jim Johnson	$20.00	$ 1.00
Valerie Leal	$20.00	$ 0.00
Vivian Vance	$20.00	$ 1.00
Julio Martinez	$40.00	$12.00
Nancy Pauls	$10.00	$ 4.00
George Moreno	$20.00	$10.00
Austin Phillips	$13.00	$ 0.00
Regina Hernandez	$10.00	$ 5.00
Annette Dolan	$40.00	$ 9.00

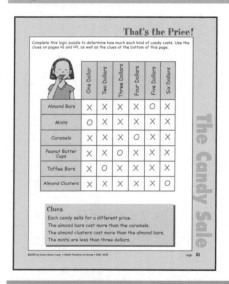

Page 51 — That's the Price!

Complete this logic puzzle to determine how much each kind of candy costs. Use the clues on pages 41 and 49, as well as the clues at the bottom of this page.

	One Dollar	Two Dollars	Three Dollars	Four Dollars	Five Dollars	Six Dollars
Almond Bars	X	X	X	X	O	X
Mints	O	X	X	X	X	X
Caramels	X	X	X	O	X	X
Peanut Butter Cups	X	X	O	X	X	X
Toffee Bars	X	O	X	X	X	X
Almond Clusters	X	X	X	X	X	O

Clues

Each candy sells for a different price.
The almond bars cost more than the caramels.
The almond clusters cost more than the almond bars.
The mints are less than three dollars.

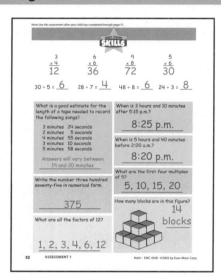

Page 52 — SKILLS Assessment 1

3	6	9	5
× 4	× 6	× 8	× 6
12	36	72	30

30 ÷ 5 = **6**　　28 ÷ 7 = **4**　　48 ÷ 8 = **6**　　24 ÷ 3 = **8**

What is a good estimate for the length of a tape needed to record the following songs?

3 minutes　24 seconds
2 minutes　5 seconds
4 minutes　55 seconds
3 minutes　10 seconds
5 minutes　58 seconds

Answers will vary between **19 and 20 minutes.**

When is 3 hours and 10 minutes after 5:15 p.m.? **8:25 p.m.**

When is 5 hours and 40 minutes before 2:00 a.m.? **8:20 p.m.**

Write the number three hundred seventy-five in numerical form. **375**

What are the first four multiples of 5? **5, 10, 15, 20**

How many blocks are in this figure? **14 blocks**

What are all the factors of 12? **1, 2, 3, 4, 6, 12**

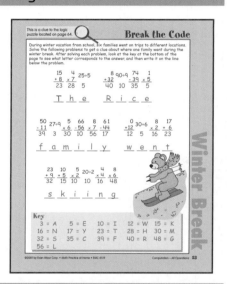

Page 53 — Break the Code

This is a clue to the logic puzzle located on page 64.
During winter vacation from school, six families went on trips to different locations. Solve the following problems to get a clue about where one family went during the winter break. After solving each problem, look at the key at the bottom of the page to see what letter corresponds to the answer, and then write it on the line below the problem.

15	4	25÷5	8	90÷9	74	1
+32	× 7		+32	-39	×5	
23	28	5	40	10	35	

T   h   e   R   i   c   e

50	27÷9	5	66	8	61	0	30÷6	8	17
-11		×6	-56	×7	-44	+12		×2	+6
39	3	30	10	56	17	12	5	16	23

f   a   m   i   l   y   w   e   n   t

23	10	5	20÷2	4	8
+9	+5	×2		×4	×6
32	15	10	10	16	48

s   k   i   i   n   g

Key

3 = A	5 = E	10 = I	12 = W	15 = K
16 = N	17 = Y	23 = T	28 = H	30 = M
32 = S	35 = C	39 = F	40 = R	48 = G
56 = L				

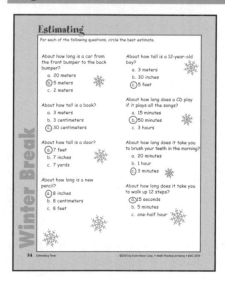

Page 54 — Estimating

For each of the following questions, circle the best estimate.

About how long is a car from the front bumper to the back bumper?
a. 20 meters
b. 5 meters
c. 2 meters

About how tall is a 12-year-old boy?
a. 3 meters
b. 30 inches
c. 5 feet

About how tall is a book?
a. 3 meters
b. 3 centimeters
c. 30 centimeters

About how long does a CD play if it plays all the songs?
a. 15 minutes
b. 50 minutes
c. 3 hours

About how tall is a door?
a. 7 feet
b. 7 inches
c. 7 yards

About how long does it take you to brush your teeth in the morning?
a. 20 minutes
b. 1 hour
c. 3 minutes

About how long is a new pencil?
a. 8 inches
b. 8 centimeters
c. 8 feet

About how long does it take you to walk up 12 steps?
a. 15 seconds
b. 5 minutes
c. one-half hour

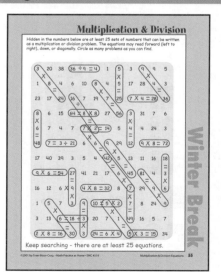

Page 55 — Multiplication & Division

Hidden in the numbers below are at least 25 sets of numbers that can be written as a multiplication or division problem. The equations may read forward (left to right), down, or diagonally. Circle as many problems as you can find.

Keep searching - there are at least 25 equations.

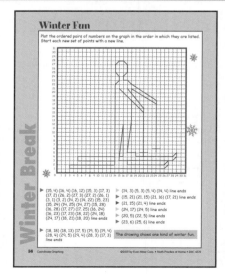

Page 56 — Winter Fun

Plot the ordered pairs of numbers on the graph in the order in which they are listed. Start each new set of points with a new line.

► (15, 4) (16, 4) (16, 12) (15, 3) (17, 3) (17, 2) (26, 2) (27, 3) (27, 2) (26, 1) (3, 12) (24, 2) (24, 22) (15, 23) (15, 24) (19, 24) (27, 25) (15, 28) (16, 28) (17, 27) (17, 25) (16, 24) (16, 23) (17, 23) (18, 22) (24, 18) (24, 17) (18, 21) (18, 20) line ends

► (34, 3) (5, 3) (5, 4) (14, 4) line ends
► (15, 21) (21, 15) (21, 16) (17, 21) line ends
► (21, 15) (21, 4) line ends
► (24, 17) (24, 5) line ends
► (20, 5) (22, 5) line ends
► (23, 6) (25, 6) line ends

► (18, 18) (18, 13) (17, 5) (19, 5) (19, 4) (28, 4) (24, 5) (25, 5) (24, 4) (28, 3) (17, 3) line ends

The drawing shows one kind of winter fun.

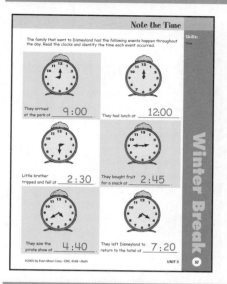

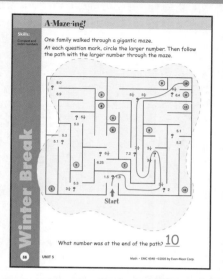

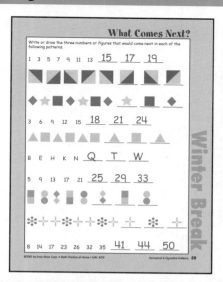

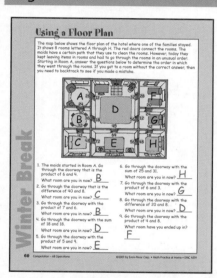

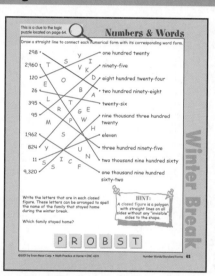

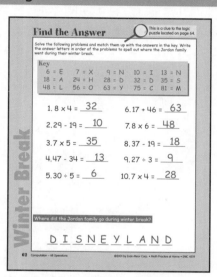

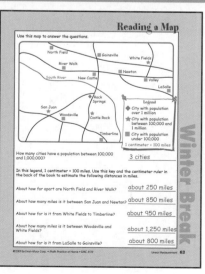

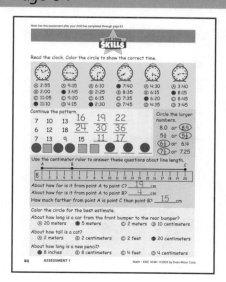

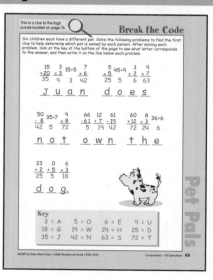

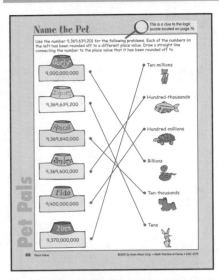

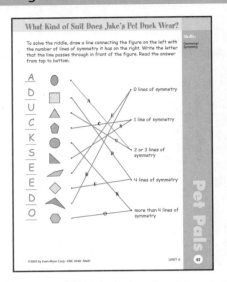

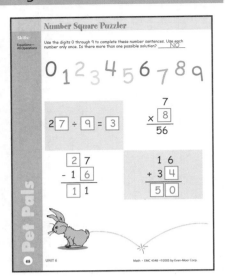

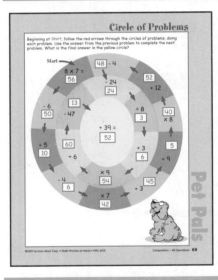

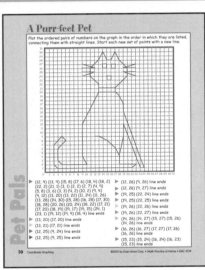

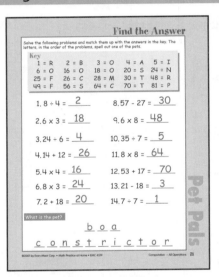

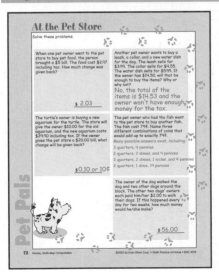

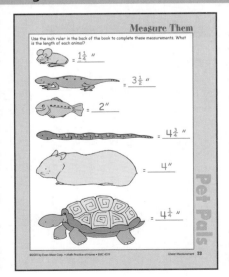

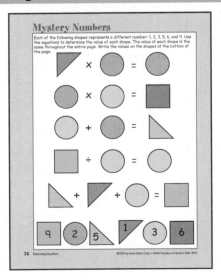

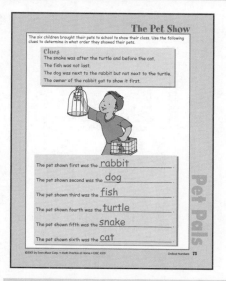

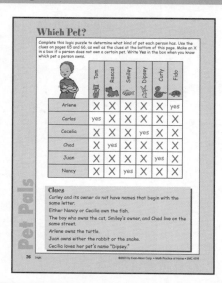

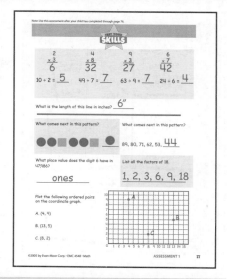

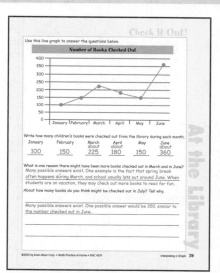

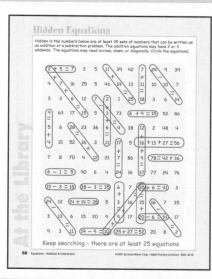

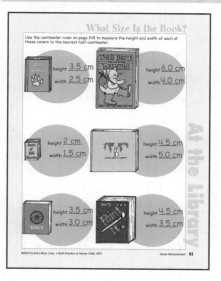

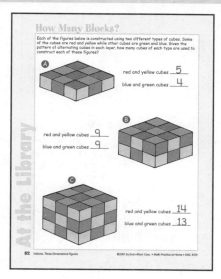

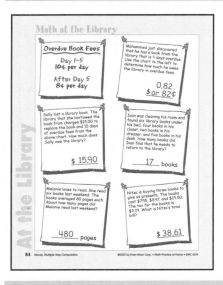

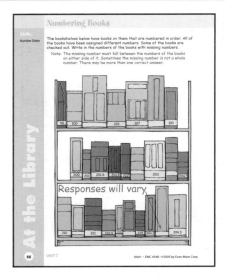

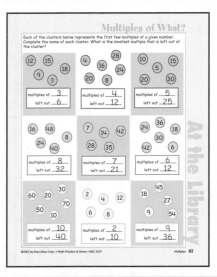

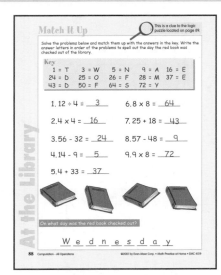

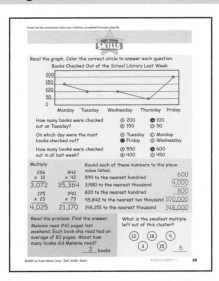

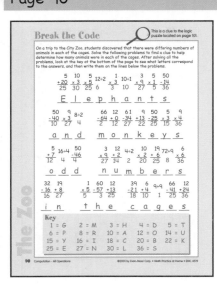

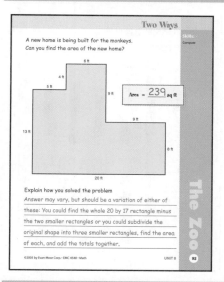

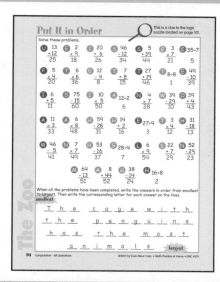

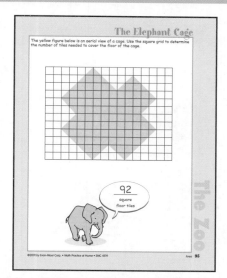

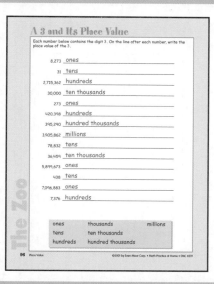

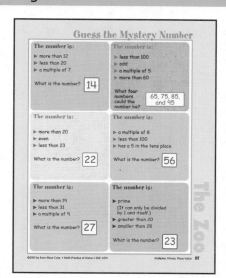

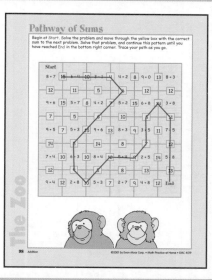

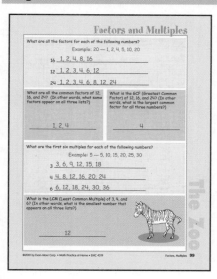

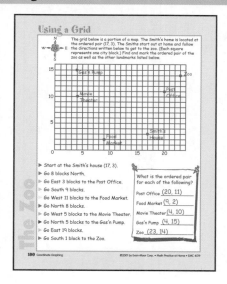

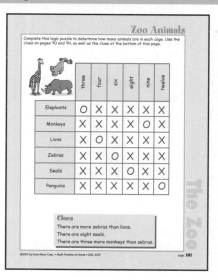

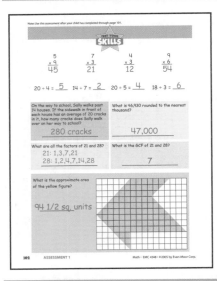

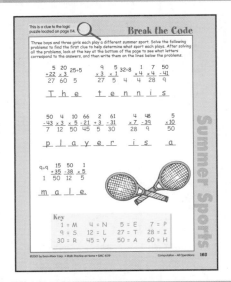

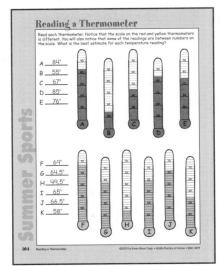

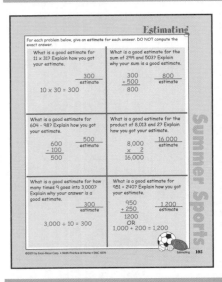

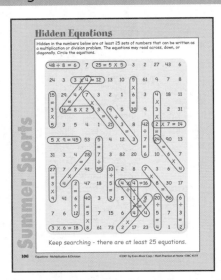

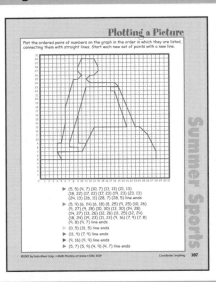

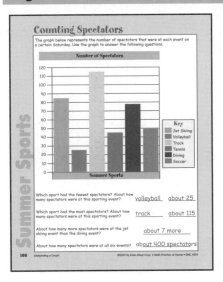

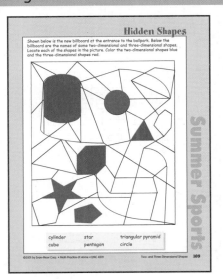

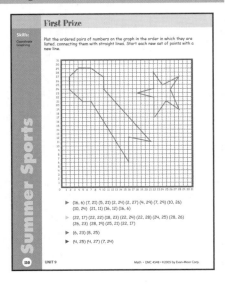

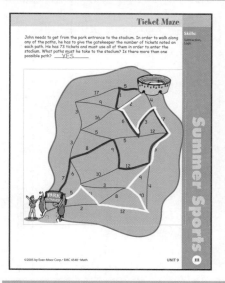

Page 111 — Ticket Maze

John needs to get from the park entrance to the stadium. In order to walk along any of the paths, he has to give the gatekeeper the number of tickets noted on each path. He has 73 tickets and must use all of them in order to enter the stadium. What paths must he take to the stadium? Is there more than one possible path? __YES__

Summer Sports

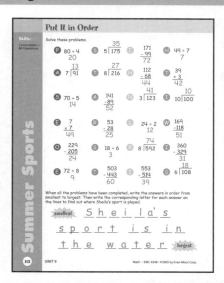

Page 112 — Put It in Order

Solve these problems.

When all the problems have been completed, write the answers in order from smallest to largest. Then write the corresponding letter for each answer on the lines to find out where Sheila's sport is played.

smallest __Sheila's__
__sport is in__
__the water__ largest

Summer Sports

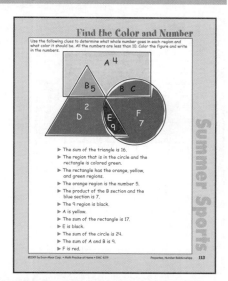

Page 113 — Find the Color and Number

Use the following clues to determine what whole number goes in each region and what color it should be. All the numbers are less than 10. Color the figure and write in the numbers.

- The sum of the triangle is 16.
- The region that is in the circle and the rectangle is colored green.
- The rectangle has the orange, yellow, and green regions.
- The orange region is the number 5.
- The product of the B section and the blue section is 7.
- The 9 region is black.
- A is yellow.
- E is black.
- The sum of the circle is 24.
- The sum of the rectangle is 17.
- The sum of A and B is 9.
- F is red.

Summer Sports

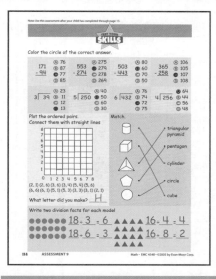

Page 114 — TEST YOUR SKILLS

Color the circle of the correct answer.

Plot the ordered pairs. Connect them with straight lines.

What letter did you make? __H__

Write two division facts for each model.
$18 \div 3 = 6$ $16 \div 4 = 4$
$18 \div 6 = 3$ $16 \div 8 = 2$

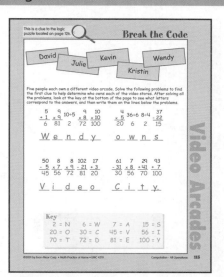

Page 115 — Break the Code

This is a clue to the logic puzzle located on page 126.

David Julie Kevin Wendy Kristin

Five people each own a different video arcade. Solve the following problems to find the first clue to help determine who owns each of the video stores. After solving all the problems, look at the key at the bottom of the page to see what letters correspond to the answers, and then write them on the lines below the problems.

__Wendy owns__

__Video City__

Key
2 = N   6 = W   7 = A   15 = S
20 = O 30 = C 45 = V   56 = I
70 = T 72 = D 81 = E 100 = Y

Video Arcades

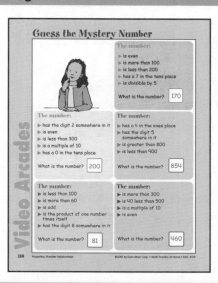

Page 116 — Guess the Mystery Number

The number:
- is even
- is more than 100
- is less than 200
- has a 7 in the tens place
- is divisible by 5
What is the number? __170__

The number:
- is even
- is less than 300
- is a multiple of 10
- has a 0 in the tens place
What is the number? __200__

The number:
- has a 4 in the ones place
- has the digit 5 somewhere in it
- is greater than 800
- is less than 900
What is the number? __854__

The number:
- is less than 100
- is more than 60
- is odd
- is the product of one number times itself
- has the digit 8 somewhere in it
What is the number? __81__

The number:
- is more than 300
- is 40 less than 500
- is a multiple of 10
- is even
What is the number? __460__

Video Arcades

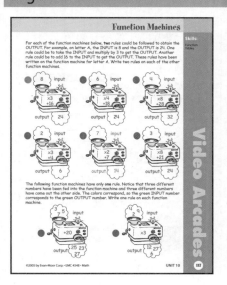

Page 117 — Function Machines

For each of the function machines below, two rules could be followed to obtain the OUTPUT. For example, on letter A, the INPUT is 8 and the OUTPUT is 24. One rule could be to take the INPUT and multiply by 3 to get the OUTPUT. Another rule could be to add 16 to the INPUT to get the OUTPUT. Write two rules on each of the other function machines.

The following function machines have only one rule. Notice that three different numbers have been fed into the function machine and three different numbers have come out the other side. The colors correspond, so the green INPUT number corresponds to the green OUTPUT number. Write one rule on each function machine.

Video Arcades

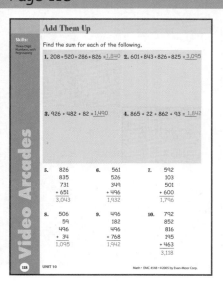

Page 118 — Add Them Up

Find the sum for each of the following.

1. $208 + 520 + 286 + 826 = 1,840$ 2. $601 + 843 + 826 + 825 = 3,095$

3. $926 + 482 + 82 = 1,490$ 4. $865 + 22 + 862 + 93 = 1,842$

5. 826
    835
    731
  + 651
    3,043

6. 561
    526
    349
  + 496
    1,932

7. 592
    103
    501
  + 600
    1,796

8. 506
    59
    496
  + 34
    1,095

9. 496
    182
    496
  + 768
    1,942

10. 792
     852
     816
     195
   + 463
     3,118

Video Arcades

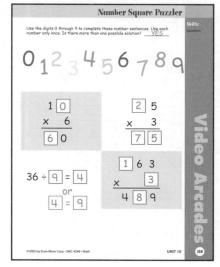

Page 119 — Number Square Puzzler

Use the digits 0 through 9 to complete these number sentences. Use each number only once. Is there more than one possible solution? __YES__

0 1 2 3 4 5 6 7 8 9

$\begin{array}{r} 1\,0 \\ \times\ 6 \\ \hline 6\,0 \end{array}$

$\begin{array}{r} 2\,5 \\ \times\ 3 \\ \hline 7\,5 \end{array}$

$36 \div 9 = 4$ or $4 \div 9$

$\begin{array}{r} 1\,6\,3 \\ \times\ 3 \\ \hline 4\,8\,9 \end{array}$

Video Arcades

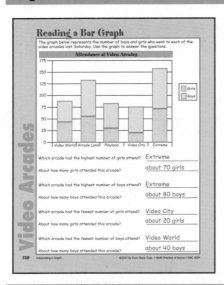

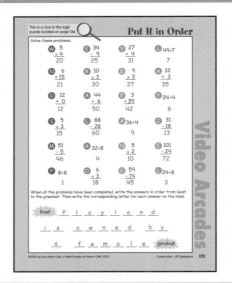

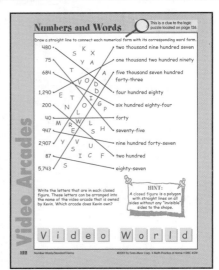

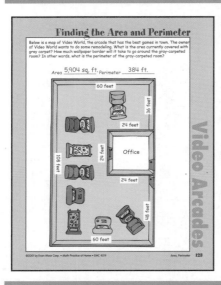

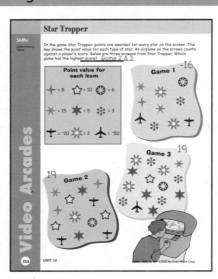

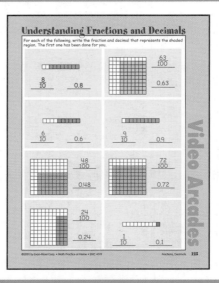

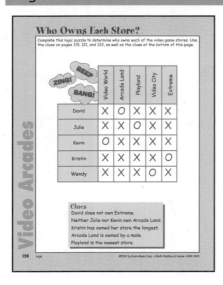

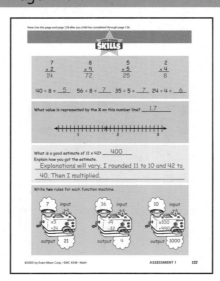

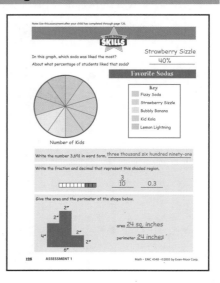